Second Shift

The **Pursuit** of
Influence
listen   love   lead ™

What Leaders are Saying about *Second Shift*

"Thought-provoking, passionate, practical—Dr. Arnold writes to the deep longing within us to live out our life's purpose. Highly recommended!"

—Marlene Bagnull, Litt.D.
Author and Director of Colorado and Philadelphia Christian Writers Conferences

"Where was this book 10 years ago? As an executive/life coach, I see many people who struggle with wanting their dream job to be their main job. What do you do when that's not possible? Through Dr. Arnold's vulnerability you feel affirmed, as though you have a trusted friend who understands your heart to operate full time in your real purpose. He 'gets you' and offers a pragmatic approach for living a life of high impact—even when your passion is on your second shift."

—Dr. Johnny Parker
Author of Exceptional Living and Former Life Coach to Washington Redskins

"Is there a dream burning inside you . . . a passion that inflames your heart? Do you long to bring it to fruition but don't know how you can do that, considering you have a day job? Dr. Arnold understands, because he was once there, too—and he knows how to help you make your dream a reality in your 'after-hours' time. Dr. Arnold's practical, God-centered advice really works and will help you bring your dream to fruition and further the glory of God's kingdom. I highly recommend this book, and I can't wait to put some of its principles into practice myself."

—Megan Breedlove,
Author of Chaotic Joy: Finding Abundance in the *Messiness of Motherhood,* and Founder of the popular MannaForMoms.com website

"Each one of us has a proverbial yellow brick road, which we MUST journey upon in order to leave our legacy. Dr. Arnold's Second Shift provides powerful insight for discovering, defending, developing, and depositing your legacy, which he masterfully describes as one's divine fingerprint. At the very time when the net worth of the personal development industry is at an all-time high, the message from this book could not be more timely."

—Dr. Ray Charles
Managing Partner of The KIIP Group, LLC, Trusted Advisor & Legacy
Coach to CEOs

"Reading Second Shift will bless you! Dr. Arnold's intriguing title (and definition of it) is explained in the context of his family history. He is transparent, sharing his struggles on his own second-shift journey. Throughout this book, Dr. Arnold cheers you on, urging and showing you how you can experience your dream life—step by step. His chapters are personal coaching sessions enabling you to achieve your goal. His insights are life-changing. Seldom do I say a book is a must read, but Second Shift is!"

—Dr. Clarence Shuler,
President and CEO of BLR: Building Lasting Relationships

"From the moment I began reading Second Shift, I wanted to take notes and absorb every word. This is not a book to be read once and set aside. Once you start, you won't stop. You will come back again and again as you fully develop into who God created you to be. Filled with relatable experiences and decades of wisdom, the practical steps are presented to inspire your potential and passion. Second Shift is an immediate classic how-to reference resource."

—Daphne V Smith
Life Coach, Speaker, and Author at www.welldonelife.com

"This is the definitive book on how to grow your part-time passion into full-time influence. Second Shift is a dream come true for people who are chasing their dream jobs. Dr. Arnold provides practical step-by-step guidelines coupled with engaging stories about how to discover and unleash your God-given purpose in ways that are eternally significant. This book is grounded in biblical truths and will inspire you to be a faithful steward of God's influence."

—Paul Sohn
Award-Winning Leadership Blogger, Author of Quarter-Life Calling

"A brilliant piece of work! The words jump off the pages and I read the entire book in three days. If you are feeling stuck and not sure which way to turn, Second Shift gives you real-life tools to understand that influence is available to anyone willing to put in the work. As I educate the masses about mental health on my day job, I can use my second shift to help women enjoy married life."

—Felicia Houston, MA, LCPC, CWA
Founder, Anointed Wives Ministry (AWM)

"Second Shift is a powerful and practical tool for anyone with a God-given desire to help others. Dr. Arnold transparently shares his own struggles and how he was able to find his voice and influence during his 'second shift.' I highly recommend this book for anyone looking to passionately pursue his or her purpose."

—Jimmy Burgess
Author of Amazon #1 Best Seller What Just Happened? How to Bounce Back in Life So You Can Do More, Have More, and Be More

"Some authors connect with readers on an emotional level, and others stimulate the reader intellectually to pursue their passions. In Second Shift, Dr. Arnold inspires you emotionally, intellectually, spiritually, and practically. Each chapter gives a clear vision of what you are currently experiencing and how you can get to the ultimate level."

—Dr. George James

Relationship & Mental Health Expert, Licensed Marriage & Family
Therapist, and CEO of George Talks LLC

"Second Shift brings a transparent—yet thought-provoking and fresh—approach to pursuing your passions and answering the call that you sense within. With precision, Dr. Arnold pushes you to not only transcend your thinking about living your passions, but also to use those passions to influence and impact others. If you are tired of pouring more energy into a 'part-time' place, this book is a must read!"

—Niki Brown

Author of There Is More! 8 Steps To Embracing The Greater You

"Second Shift's magnificent aim is to liberate and propel the minds of our era into complete confidence that cultural influence is possible while on your 'second shift.' This book is a must read!!"

—Dr. Gilbert Coleman

Senior Pastor, Freedom Christian Bible Fellowship
and Overseer of Freedom Worldwide Covenant Ministries

"Dr. Arnold is a man on a mission using his own 'second shift' to change lives. This book will not only help you master your margins, but define your load and slay your DRAGONS. Enjoy the journey."

—Chris Richardson

Relationship Strategist and Host of the Real Talk with Chris Richardson
Radio Show

Second Shift

How to Grow Your Part-Time Passion to Full-Time Influence

Dr. Harold Arnold, Jr.

Second Shift: How to Grow your Part-Time Passion to Full-Time Influence
First Edition, March 2016

Author: Dr. Harold Arnold, Jr.
Editor: Melissa Peitch
Cover: Kiryl Lysenka

Copyright © 2015 Harold Arnold
Print Edition
ISBN-10: 1522842098
ISBN-13: 978-1-5228-4209-5

CONTENTS

ACKNOWLEDGMENTS

Over the years many people have meaningfully contributed to my second-shift successes. But, three have most demonstrated to me a lifetime of commitment to second-shift influence.

For nearly my entire life, I have watched my father—the Reverend Harold L. Arnold, Sr.—serve God through pastoring. After working one and sometimes two day jobs with barely any sleep, he pushed through his physical limitations to impart the Word of God. It never mattered to my father whether there were one or one hundred people in the pews. For my father, pastoring on the second shift spanned more than forty years without regard for the meager pay or social status. On those nights when I have been physically exhausted and emotionally dispirited, I remember how he never complained. So, neither will I.

My mother, Dorothy P. Arnold, is another model of second shift service. Whether it was fostering dozens of children over many years, creating side hustles to earn extra money, or actively supporting the business endeavors of her children, she never stops pushing. She constantly pushes through physical and mental pain to pursue her goals. On those nights that my mind wants to quit, I remember that my mom has pushed through much worse. So must I.

Finally, I must acknowledge my dear wife, Dalia Ward Arnold, who has encouraged and endured my pursuit of influence on the second shift when it has inevitably impinged upon our family time. Without her, my second shift would be meaningless. More than anything else, I want her to know that she is the wind beneath my wings. She should know that any second-shift influence that I have achieved is equally hers to claim.

1

FOREWORD

"I get it!" I exclaimed to my good friend, Dr. Arnold as soon as he told me the title of this book during its early stages. I told him there was no need for further explanation. I immediately understood the term "second shift," because I've lived it my entire life . . . and you probably have, too. The second shift is where your passion intersects with your God-given purpose. That's why you're able to work a demanding 9 to 5, take care of your children, and do other countless tasks before your second shift even starts.

I know this all too well from my own experience on the second shift. My wife Ronnie and I worked two very demanding day jobs in Information Technology, but at night, we worked towards the primary purpose that God had for our lives. After a full day of working at our day jobs, a 1.5-hour commute, dinner time, and bed time, our second shift would be just getting started. By the time the second shift kicked off, it was already 9 or 10 PM, and by the time we were able to rest—if there was rest that evening—it would be 2 or 3 AM. The only thing that kept us moving forward was our passion that pushed us towards our purpose.

No credible voice will tell you it is easy. But, over the past eight years, we have been humbled to watch what started (on the second shift) as a personal blog grow into an international brand under our own Tyler New Media umbrella—which also boasts five independently produced films and a social media presence that includes over eleven million total readers and 500,000 Facebook fans. Such is the power of passion.

Too many times, I've heard others explain away passion as if it isn't important to reaching success—whether that success stems from obtaining a degree, reaching a fitness goal, or starting a business. But, I've realized that passion is paramount.

What exactly does that passion look and feel like? That passion is the burst of energy that allows you to keep moving forward, following your dreams and desires when you feel like giving up. Without that passion, you're bound to quit and add another task to a list of items you've started without completion. So, passion must be present. What happens when your passion leads you to your purpose? The physical manifestation of your hard work results in your influence.

In the pages of this book, Dr. Arnold walks you through the various stages of influence that you'll face, and provides a blueprint for how to handle each one. Once you are equipped with these tools, you'll have what you need to harness true success on your own second shift journey. Dr. Arnold is the perfect person to mentor you in this area, because his leadership is evident to anyone who has ever seen him in action. From the very first time that we met, at a retreat for marriage leaders, it was evident. Since then, I've seen him exhibit his influence as a minister, professional, and entrepreneur. Who better to take you on this journey than a leader amongst leaders?

This is your opportunity to learn how to follow your passion to your purpose and leverage that into the power of influence. Then, watch that influence manifest into the different areas of your life and the lives of those around you. What you'll quickly find is that the best and most beneficial way to wield influence is through service. By serving others, you unlock your greatest gift. When you serve others, you see your business explode and you see the world around you begin to shift. And the more you serve others, the more growth you'll see.

I'm excited about your journey through this book. Don't take this opportunity lightly. This is your opportunity to harness your full potential . . . but only if you strategically follow along with the information, and then implement what you learn. True passion always becomes action. Without action, you won't see the second shift results and payout in your own life. Consume the information. Follow the blueprint. Step into your purpose.

Lamar Tyler
Co-founder Tyler New Media
BlackandMarriedWithKids.com
2012 Ebony Power 100 Honoree—2014 Black Enterprise Family Business of the Year Finalist

PREFACE

I was born to write this book—I really believe that. The more I think about my life's journey, the more I am convinced that it led me here. This book is instructive, helping one to look at the patterns of one's life and derive meaning from it. As I reflect back, over nearly thirty years since I completed my undergraduate degree at Howard University, I see one consistent pattern in the midst of life's twists. I have nearly always worked the second shift. What do I mean by the second shift?

For years, I never had a term to describe the many semesters of graduate school, litany of civic and service appointments, enormous ministry responsibilities, and building of my own business platform that were all done after finishing my work at my day job. This balancing act also included being a husband and father for nearly all of those years. A few years ago, it dawned on me. All of these are things that I do to give me that sense of fulfillment—almost like having another job. And, there it was, clear as day. I was working the second shift. Somehow just putting this label on these diverse episodes of my life makes my life feel more official and cohesive—like it was all pointing to a singular destination, or that there was a common thread connecting the dots.

As I have intentionally reflected over the years on my second shift, I have arrived at a conclusion: My second shift has effectively been a career. My vocation in Information Technology lasted fifteen years. My tenure as a Market Researcher has been more than eleven years. Together, my two traditional careers have transpired over a twenty-six-year period. But, my career on the second shift alone has been even longer than those traditional careers combined. There are probably a number of narratives that I could use to synthesize the countless nights taking classes for graduate school, the hundreds of hours working to empower disenfranchised individuals, the hundreds of counseling hours that I have logged, and the dozens of ministry leadership positions I have held. But, I wondered, is there a unifying narrative? I had some ideas.

One day while sitting with branding expert, Dick Bruso of Heard Above the Noise, it all crystallized for me. After mulling over my full body of work, Dick said, "Your life has been about influence." I thought about it for a moment. A moment is all it took; it immediately resonated. I knew it was true. I quickly scanned back over the events of my life. Why did I move my family three thousand miles to pursue a degree in Marriage and Family Therapy, although my career was in technology? Why did I serve as volunteer Director of Education for a large multi-cultural church? Why did I design and oversee, as well as serve as counselor for, a robust lay counseling program? Why did I complete two Master's degrees in the behavioral sciences and a Ph.D. in Psychology? Dick's words struck my core. All of the years of struggling and pushing myself had a purpose.

All of the psychological, relational, spiritual, and financial strain had transcendent meaning. It all pointed towards influence. But, that influence was not a destination that I had reached—that much is clear. It is a process, a journey. Now, I think of it as a pursuit of influence. My thirty-year career on the second shift has been about the pursuit of influence—becoming someone who helps people in their times of need. However, what I did not realize as clearly was that the second shift was really about God meeting me at my point of need. The second shift has been a spiritual, psychological, relational, and vocational process of molding me into the person that lives and shares life to the fullest.

For many years, I fought the idea that the second shift was my platform for influence. I, like so many others, wanted to pursue my passions as my day job. I desired to find a means of earning a living that did not require me to feel like I was just going through the motions for a paycheck. I wanted to stop dreading Monday mornings. I looked forward to a day when I wasn't dreaming of the weekend by Tuesday afternoon. For many years, I blamed my day job for my discontent. In my mind, my job was what was standing between me and my true destiny. When I felt I was treated unfairly by a client or my co-workers, that seemed to be proof that I was in the wrong place. While I wanted to be a professional and produce excellent quality work for my clients, I knew that I was not giving my demanding day jobs one hundred percent. I felt that I needed to have something left for my passionate pursuits after hours. And, over time, it became increasingly difficult to keep the juggling act going.

I prayed, cried, networked, and sometimes job searched, all in an effort to make my day job and my dream job one in the same. But, everything seemed to be a dead end. With five degrees, many years of experience, and a talent for client interaction, it was baffling how much trouble I had even finding a job to which I wanted to apply. After one particular discussion with a friend of mine who is talented in strategic management, everything came to a head. She asked me to outline what type of tasks I imagine myself doing at my dream job. As I contemplated this, I realized why I was having such difficulty finding my dream job. The bottom line is that my dream job was not going to be found in a corporate job description, help wanted ads, or executive search firm solicitations. No—my dream job needed to be created . . . and that scared me most of all.

I wanted to find a place that would hire me and give me a predictable (and substantial) income to perform what I most enjoyed—authentically connecting with people across cultures and empowering them to live their fullest life in relation to those around them. But, for years, nothing seemed to really change, other than my increasing sense of futility that this was ever going to happen. Though I sincerely felt that God had directed the major steps of my life, the constant doubts and frustrations were getting the best of me. Though I was proud of the work that I had done in the years of passionate pursuits, I felt like a coward and a failure that I had not obtained that dream job. Maybe I just wasn't good enough, courageous enough, or full of enough faith to have the dream job that seemed so accessible to others. Maybe, I thought, this is as good as it gets for me. However, things were about to get very interesting.

THE BREAKTHROUGH

I never wanted to be a vegetarian. After all, I wore my love for meat as a badge of honor—like most Southern boys do. But, desperation causes one to do uncommon things. For several years, I had wanted more clarity of direction, more reach for my voice, and more open doors for my passions. Yes, I experienced some successes, but my breakthrough always felt just out of reach. I felt I was at a psychological and emotional impasse. The time for change was now . . . but only if God would show me the way.

It was the last day of a marriage retreat in Montego Bay, Jamaica, at which my wife Dalia and I were presenting with several others. The final presenter, Pastor Jamaal Bernard, issued an impassioned challenge to all of us: "How desperate are you?"[1] His question evoked a strong, visceral response within me about my passion portfolio—my purpose for being in this world. Tired of feeling as if my options were limited, I internalized this challenge as a personal call to action. I was getting desperate. It's cliché, but "desperate times do call for desperate measures."

During my trip back home from Jamaica, I began to sense my response to Pastor Bernard's challenge. I needed a way to lean in

---

[1] Bernard, J., "How desperate are you?" Christian Cultural Center Marriage Retreat, Rose Hall, Jamaica. 2013.

to God and focus on hearing His voice. I felt called to what is called a "fast"—a biblical tradition of consecrating oneself by sacrificing elements of one's regular diet. For me, the message felt clear. Give up what you like most—meat. All of it. (Yes, even fish and seafood.) It felt extreme, but it also felt right. I went back to God once more, but this time with a passionate plea, reminiscent of the biblical account of Jacob in the book of Genesis. I prayed, "God, I will not eat meat again until I receive my breakthrough." And, so with both desperation and resolution, my journey began.

To my amazement, that vegetarian experience lasted for twelve months and it transformed me in innumerable ways. I achieved that breakthrough that I sought (though not quite in the way that I expected). During this period, my mind was expanded to learn how to develop my voice to speak from a place of passion, and how to build a platform over which that voice can actually be heard. In very practical ways, this vegetarian journey was the catalyst for themes that you will experience in this book.

As I survey my body of work since my own breakthrough experience, one thing has been clear above everything else: obedience to our unique calling means realizing that we must authentically integrate all of the aspects of ourselves and then give that away to enrich others' lives. I coined the phrase "see more to know more to be more to live more to give more" to capture the sense in which the things that enrich us are intended to transform others as well. This is the meaning of influence at its most basic. And, sometimes when we are feeling most defeated, God allows a circumstance to arise that restores your sense of confidence that you are indeed moving in the right direction—even when it doesn't feel like it.

THE CALL OF INFLUENCE

Not too long ago, at a time when I needed it most, the undulating vibration of my cell phone was about to momentarily repel my own demons of doubt. The display flashed an unfamiliar number from North Carolina. I answered. A woman asked for me by name. To her surprise, I assured her that she had indeed reached me directly. She thanked me for taking her call and then got right to the point.

She talked about the difficulty of being a single, African-American mother and having a conversation with her teenage son about staying sexually abstinent until marriage. She wanted a way to talk about it with him from a Christian perspective. But, she didn't know where to start. She did what we all do: turn to Google. During her Google search, she discovered a blog post that I had written months earlier titled, "10 Reasons I'm Glad I was a Virgin When I Married." She was flabbergasted that a male, and an African-American one at that, wrote such an article. She had struck gold and wanted to personally thank me for writing it.

She described how she sat down with her son and simply went through the different points of the article. As I listened to her, I simultaneously felt a sense of joy and pride that I was able to add value to this mom's life. Little did I know she was not done.

She suddenly asked, "Will you talk to my son? I want him to really know that there is a Black man out there that really did this. I want him to know that you exist for real. I'm not making this up."

What was I to say other than, "Well sure. Put him on."

Over the next fifteen minutes, I was able to connect with the young man. Of course, he was initially tepid, but gradually opened up. I remember his first question, "What did you say when guys were talking about being with girls?" Then, I knew he was invested in the conversation. He was listening.

The second shift, especially in the early years of platform building, is rife with the feeling of obscurity. It just feels like no one is listening. That hurts when you know that you are putting your best self out there. We really just want to know that someone is listening. Here was a mom that had listened. There I was, talking to her teenage son, who was listening. Despite the doubts that sometimes go through my mind and make me question the effectiveness of my efforts, this mom and her son were influenced by my voice. This teenager, without really knowing me, was willing to be vulnerable and ask for my help in responding to one of his real-life problems. This is influence. That mother and son will probably never know how much they blessed me that day. She called to thank me, but I felt like I should be the one thanking her for reminding me to be faithful to my passion. God will provide the increase—much of which I will never physically see. Just remember, sometimes influence manifests in unexpected ways.

I have received many calls from people who have read articles that I have written, or my book, *Marriage ROCKS for Christian Couples*,[2] or who maybe have attended one of my seminars or retreats. But, that day I learned a lesson that has stayed with me. It is hard to put my finger on exactly what made this call so impactful. I think, however, that a shift occurred . . . from hoping that I was making a difference, to knowing that I was.

I knew the mom had found the help she needed. I knew that my writing brought a mother and her son together. I knew that her son trusted me, a stranger, to give him guidance on a

---

[2] Arnold, H., Ph.D., *Marriage ROCKS for Christian Couples*. 2009: Judson Press.

difficult subject. That day of the call, three things crystallized in my spirit.

First, doubt and self-limiting beliefs are the enemy of influence because they plant the seeds of failure where it matters most—in your mind. Second, even when I cannot see it, I must trust that my best offerings will make a tangible difference in someone's life. Trust is influence's ally, fertilizing and watering it, allowing it to yield the fruit of success. Third, passion is not something that you pursue in the abstract. That day, I saw passion as "Pass-I-On"—passing on what God put in you to another. Whether pursued as your day job or your dream job—or both—passion is personal.

JARS OF CLAY

To be perfectly transparent, when I first set out to write this book I wanted it to speak equally to people of faith and those with a more secular orientation. However, I quickly encountered a problem. While I think all of these principles apply to both groups of people, I struggled to speak of transcendent meaning without invoking my belief that God has a divine purpose for my life and yours. I hesitate to even think about life's meaning apart from a spiritual compass that directs me and helps me discern my own wants from God's call on my life. The more this realization sinks into my spirit, the more I understand that the second shift is a spiritual workshop—a place where we are each masterfully shaped into vessels of honor. God is that master craftsman who fuses our life experiences with a divine calling that oftentimes must be pursued through non-traditional means.

Throughout this book, I invoke the Apostle Paul's letters to the early Christian churches because they speak so powerfully to the perils and joys that we all experience when living our calling. As I reflect on my second shift journey—especially its low points—I am encouraged by Paul's words to the Corinthian church, "But we have this treasure in jars of clay, to show that the surpassing power belongs to God and not to us" (2 Corinthians 4:7).

Despite the fragility we feel on the second shift, Paul affirms our resilience in noting how "we are afflicted in every way, but not crushed; perplexed, but not driven to despair; persecuted, but not forsaken; struck down, but not destroyed" (2 Corinthians 4:8-9). How can clay jars command such power? As Paul says, it is only as we understand "the surpassing power belongs to God and not us." As a jar of clay, you see that the second shift is about God, not about you. You do not have what it takes to sustain second-shift mastery using your own strength, only God's. You do not have enough hours to reach all of the people you need to touch. But, God redeems the time. Your second shift is proof that what God began in you is neither crushed nor destroyed. The key, however, is to pursue your specific call at your very own pace.

There is no universally right pace; there is only your pace. And, your pace is different than mine. We cannot compare our respective paces; we can only encourage one another to run his or her race. Having been a runner for nearly fifteen years, there is one thing I know: you cannot run someone else's pace for very long. If you want a sustained effort, you have to focus on running your own race. Yet, how many of us spend too much energy comparing our progress in business, ministry, and life with others who appear to be so much further along? We get caught in the trap of comparing our beginning to someone else's ending. We get dispirited when we feel that we cannot keep up. This comparison quandary is particularly dangerous for those of us who pursue our passions in the margins of our lives. Maybe that was why it was so liberating for me to internalize this idea that obedience to my purpose for which I was built is simply to "Pass-I-On" — my influence at my own pace.

PREFACE

This book is intended to help you find your own pace, especially for those of us whose passion is not pursued or fulfilled during our day job. Each chapter introduces you to key concepts, anecdotes, and practical tips for running your best race, touching lives along your path, and most of all remembering that you are a treasured jar of clay.

On your mark. Get set. Go!

PART 1:

THE PURSUIT OF INFLUENCE

CHAPTER 1

CREATED FOR INFLUENCE

"Think twice before you speak, because your words and influence will plant the seed of either success or failure in the mind of another."

- NAPOLEON HILL

The greatest human desire is to passionately weave meaning into one's life story and, in the process, discover the thread that connects to another. This connective thread, called influence, is the tie that binds us to our Creator, our community, and our call. Like the intricate design of a spider's silken web, your strands of influence form a relational network with the power to capture the hearts and minds of culture. Your relational web of influence is your access to the greatest wealth imaginable.

This is a book about wealth—but not primarily the financial type. In the 21st century, money is no longer the sole (or maybe even primary) measure of wealth. Rather, wealth today is measured by influence. It is the currency of our age. Arguably, that has been the case in every century, but it is incontrovertible today. The financially wealthy, unlike many of us of more modest means, pedal influence—not money. They understand that it isn't the money that creates the power. Rather, it is the power and influence that create the money. Those among the upper financial echelon know that true power lies in the breadth of one's influence. For them, money is simply a byproduct of such influence. This is an important distinction because it determines one's starting point. The wealthy focus on solidifying their base of influence—often taking on substantial "risks" to do so. The rest of us attempt to first establish a solid financial footing—only to be frustrated by the way expenses always seem to outpace the revenue. But, because influence is their starting point, the wealthiest individuals don't think about risk the same way as the rest of us. Rather than thinking of money as a finite resource to be conserved, the wealthiest individuals believe there is an almost inexhaustible supply. Money can be created—not with a printing press, but with access to influential people, places, and things. This quid pro quo exchange among the traditional influencers left the rest of us outside the gate, looking in—wishing, waiting, and wondering when, if ever, our time would come.

But, things are now different. Extraordinary influence is no longer reserved for a privileged few—no longer the exclusive domain of the rich or well connected. Influence is no longer dictated by media moguls, political pundits, and exclusive societies. Thank God. Their monopolistic reign is over. Now, it's your time. Your dream to positively impact lives at home, work, church, and across the global community can happen today at a level previously unimaginable. For the first time in human history, your vision can explode from concept to global relevance in days—not years, or even months. Your extraordinary influence simply depends on the creative vitality of your message, the force of your personality, and the boldness of your imagination. Imagination's relevance cannot be overstated. Simply put, your imagination—more than any other factor—forms the perimeter of your purpose. If you can visualize it, you can achieve it.

But, therein lies a problem. Many of us struggle to visualize having extraordinary influence. We see others attain it, but it feels too distant for us personally. That has been the frustration of my own journey. Even with all of my successes, I feel like an underachiever because my passions feel part-time. I do not mean to say that I feel my passions are marginalized; in fact, they swell within me every single day. Every day, my passion pushes me to imagine creative ideas that intrigue. Every day, my passion conjures ways that I can add value to the lives of others. But, for some, part-time passion feels like partial fulfillment. It is the stark and sometimes sad reality that I have to entertain and pursue these passions in the discretionary, rather than primary, portions of my day. If that is your story too, then this book is for you.

After a long day in the office—often dealing with complicated projects, difficult people, impossible timelines, and ten-hour-plus work days—we must summon the energy for our passions. Are our passions being cheated of our best self? It sure feels like it. We wonder what we might achieve if our passions could be pursued full-time. Could we write more books? Would we have a larger network of connections? How much money could we make? These thoughts, and many others, swarm in our minds constantly—especially when we listen to the stories of those who are pursuing their passions as their vocation.

Personally, I am not jealous of them at all. In fact, I admire them. If I'm being honest, I can admit that I feel a profound sense of disappointment in myself. Why can I not take that leap? Is it a lack of faith that stands between me and my potential? Would I have more influence if I just threw caution to the wind? Must my passions be content with my leftovers? You may have asked yourself these same questions.

> **While our imagination forms the perimeter of our purpose, our fears are its drain.**

The answer feels complicated and paralyzing. It's both rational and emotional. Ultimately, however, I have come to a conclusion about myself and others—maybe even you. While our imagination forms the perimeter of our purpose, our fears are its drain. I can point to rational and irrational justification for that fear within myself, but it all boils down to fear. Fear of financial failure, fear of pursuing my passions full-time before I have positioned my wife to do the same, and a simple fear of uncertainty. I am afraid to leap.

The dreaded fear of uncertainty has stifled the dreams of many would-be influencers from the beginning of mankind until today. I am certainly not alone in my hesitation to whole-heartedly leap into God's promises for me—especially when the outcome seems unclear. When I honestly examine my own fears, I get a glimpse into the plight of the Children of Israel as they wandered haplessly in the wilderness for forty years rather than claiming the Promised Land that God had already prepared for them. Paralyzed by the spies' majority report that the Promised Land was not accessible because of the giants who occupied it, the Hebrews' fear overwhelmed their faith. They were afraid to leap into a plan that God had to place His people at the center of what, unbeknownst to them, would be a major trade and cultural exchange route that would influence the known world for generations. Then and now, God wants His people positioned at the cultural crossroads to influence the world with His kingdom message. You and I were created for kingdom influence.

THE INFLUENCE PROFESSIONAL

My friend, Kary Oberbrunner, suggests nine steps to becoming an influence peddler in his excellent book, *Day Job to*

Dream Job.[3] Many are flocking to the notion of pursuing that dream job, because his model makes it sound attainable for anyone. For those of us burgeoning with those part-time passions, the idea of that dream job seems like nirvana. Everyone's dream job looks a little different, but all of those dream jobs share a common component—they represent a liberation of our passions. And, for many, that liberation means more influence. More specifically, it means full-time influence. Or so we imagine.

I have heard successful entrepreneurs and bestselling authors like Michael Hyatt (*Platform: Get Noticed in a Noisy World*),[4] Jeff Goins (*The Art of Work*),[5] and many others refer to this dedicated, full-time pursuit of one's dream as "going PRO." It is a clever, catchy phrase. Somehow, however, it leaves me feeling cheated, as if the rest of us who work non-stop to make our dreams a reality are amateurs. Though I know it is not their intention, somehow "going PRO" seems to imply that my influence is somehow amateurish.

I know that your influence and mine are not the stuff of novices. Yes, I may have to pursue my passions part-time in this season. But, I offer professional quality value. Just today, I received a message from a woman in Florida. She met me during a marriage conference at which I spoke more than a year ago. Today, she asked me how she can heal from the wound of her husband's infidelity. She is not looking for an amateur response. She needs hope and encouragement from a trusted and informed source who cares. That is what I offered her.

For me, a more accurate depiction of "going PRO" is engendering trust, offering valuable content, and—most of all—

[3] Oberbrunner, K., *Day Job to Dream Job: Practical Steps for Turning Your Passion into a Full-Time Gig.* 2014: Baker Books.
[4] Hyatt, M., Platform: *Get Noticed in a Noisy World.* 2012: Thomas Nelson.
[5] Goins, J., *The Art of Work: A Proven Path to Discovering What You Were Meant to Do.* 2015: Thomas Nelson.

caring deeply. Any area in which you demonstrate those three qualities, you are a professional, because you are compensated in the currency of the new economy: Influence.

I've been using this term, "full-time influence." But, what does it really mean? Some mistakenly think of full-time influence as the number of hours that you cultivate your passion in a day. When they are unable to allocate a large portion of their day to their passion, they think full-time influence is unachievable. Others misinterpret full-time influence to imply some minimum number of people reached by your message or product. Full-time influence is neither of these. So, what is it?

> **Full-time influence is your passion's fullest potential for good among the broadest range of people in your path.**

Simply put, full-time influence is your passion's fullest potential for good among the broadest range of people in your path. Full-time influence in your area of passion is going to be different than mine, because your potential is different than mine. Some people have more innate or developed talent in their area of passion than others. So, their influence may have more potential. But, this does not diminish your ability to have full-time influence. Others' paths may be wider or less bumpy than yours. Again, this does not preclude you from having full-time influence. This is why it is so important that we avoid the comparison trap. Full-time influence is personal to your span of ability and reach.

It is equally important to remember that not everyone desires to maximize or to have full-time influence. Some people are content with living a good life of positive influence on family and close friends, without the dream for something bigger. If that is you, then I would like to affirm you. The greatest place for anyone's influence is in the home and among those who are most important to you. Exerting influence on these select groups is vital and life changing for them, and also for you. I believe that there are components of this book that are going to help you in these endeavors. But, if you dream of an even greater impact, then this book is tailored for you.

Many resources are available, both in bookstores and all across the Internet, on how to pursue your dream as your full-time endeavor. Online forums and blogs abound with hundreds of thousands of people seeking to abandon their day job to heed the call of their passions. It sounds sexy. It appeals to our innermost being. We feel warm all over just thinking about the possibilities. This makes perfect sense, because this idea of making your dreams of influence a reality is what you were created to do—you were created for influence.

I admit that I fantasize about what it would mean to pursue the full liberation of my passions, too. But, I also offer a word of caution because we must be very careful with the assumptions that we allow ourselves to believe. Many marketing and "get rich quick" pundits hope to capitalize on (or in some cases exploit) your hopes and dreams with promises of lofty benefits, unparalleled growth, and immediate access that you can gain usually by purchasing their latest once-in-a-lifetime product. Be a wise consumer and exercise prudence towards most of these pitches—many of them empty and with their own trail of dissatisfied people with dashed hopes.

Despite what the gurus may say, not everyone is in a position to make their dream job their day job—at least not right now. Any credible source will tell you that overnight success is a myth 99.9% of the time. Unfortunately, the idea appeals to our senses (though our sensibilities should tell us otherwise). For most of us, this conversion is a process, and you'll need a training ground. This book does not guarantee you success or suggest some "secret sauce" that will open your door to treasure or immediate influence. But, what it does promise is affirmation that you really can cultivate and grow your passions. If you so desire, in time, you can be in a position to liberate your passions full-time. But, until that time, you have the tools at your disposal to grow your part-time passions to full-time influence. If your desire is full-time influence, you do not have to wait for your break from your day job—or what I call your first shift. You, my friend, were created for influence. Like the fabled pot of gold at the end of the rainbow, your passion always leads to your influence.

SECOND SHIFT: YOUR GATEWAY TO INFLUENCE

I have personally never done what is conventionally called "shift work." I did, however, grow up in a home and a blue-collar town where it was the predominant mode of work. Shift work is an employment practice in which the day is divided into "shifts"— set periods of time during which different groups of workers take up their posts. The term "shift work" includes both long-term night shifts and work schedules in which employees change or rotate shifts.

For our purposes, we think of the first shift as that period of time and set of responsibilities that occupy the largest portion of your day. Using myself as an example, I typically report to my day job in pharmaceutical market research on weekdays from 8:30 a.m. to 6:00 p.m. The nature of my job, however, demands that I do whatever it takes to get the job done. Sometimes, I can get things accomplished in a regular forty-hour week. Other times, it may take fifty or more. My first shift is primarily filled with helping my pharmaceutical clients to position their products and services with healthcare professionals and consumers. It is a demanding job with high expectations. Do it cheaper. Get it done faster. That is the nature of the current environment in pharmaceutical market research. That is my first shift. Your first shift probably looks different.

I need to make one point clear. The first shift is not about the time of day that you work, the type of work that you do, or even the amount of money that you make—although these are obvious facets of one's first shift. For our purposes, however, the first shift represents the period of your time that you must directly allocate to the primary responsibilities of life. For nearly thirty years, the first shift has been my secular vocation, but not my vision. Honestly, over the years this incongruity has left me sad. I remember days as far back as my twenties, when I sat in my car in the parking lot of IBM (my first job out of college) and literally cried because I did not want to walk in the building. There have been days when I have stood in the shower in tears as I prepared to go to my first shift, because it seemed so distant from what I felt called to do.

Here is one thing I know: You have been there, too. In fact, you may be there right now. I understand. In some ways, I always feel caught in that tension. The responsibility of the first shift tugs you one way, while the call of passion seems to pull you in a different direction. These are the difficult days when your dreams feel like fantasies and your passions seem passive. When you struggle to move the needle on your passion, the disappointment and depression can be paralyzing. On top of that, the demands of the first shift seem to constantly increase. The result can be catastrophic. For peace of mind, many people give up their passion and settle into life's comfort zone to ease the feeling of failure. The flame which once burned bright within them is reduced to smoldering embers. They feel defeated.

My promise to you is that your first-shift responsibilities never need be so demanding that your passions and influence are muted. Yes, some people are fortunate or blessed to have a passion that they do full-time or as their day's primary focus. Whether through privilege, courageous faith, simple determination, or other avenue, these people have positioned themselves to spend the bulk of their day doing what they love. I call them "first-shifters." The first-shifters love their day jobs and leverage these vocations to pursue their passions. The benefit for first-shifters is their ability to prioritize their passion at their discretion. It may be the nurse who can think of nothing she enjoys more than treating sick children at the hospital's pediatric unit on her first shift. Or, I think of my friend Bob Oliver, a pharmaceutical executive who has risen to the position of President of Marketing for a major pharmaceutical company and sees his first shift as an opportunity to demonstrate wholehearted leadership to the organization. It could be like Lamar and Ronnie Tyler, who on their first shift, have built an online presence at Blackandmarriedwithkids.com that, in 2011 and 2012, placed them among Ebony magazine's Power 100 (a list of the top 100 movers and shakers in the Black community) and in 2015 positioned them as finalists in InfusionSoft's small business competition.[6] These first-shifters have aligned their vision and their vocation.

Unfortunately, that has not been my path or that of most other passionate dreamers that I personally know. No, our passion is presently pursued in the margins of our lives. It is those evenings from 7:00 p.m. to midnight on most weekdays, and at least three to four hours on Saturday or Sunday. It is the first-shift lunch breaks that are used to sketch some of my ideas for influence on the back of an envelope. It is the vacation hours that are used from my first shift to conduct speaking engagements in my area of passion. It is the countless emails that are sent to make connections, answer questions, and seek partnerships in my area of passion. It is the phone calls for help that I receive on my personal cell when I am frantically juggling

---

[6] Lamar and Ronnie Tyler [cited 2015]; Available from: https://blackandmarriedwithkids.com/about-us/

the responsibilities of my day job. It is the money that I spend to read more books, join more communities, and build an online platform in an effort to create more value for people and have more influence.

I know that I am not alone. The fact that you are reading this book is proof of that. You also are in pursuit of influence after your first-shift obligations are done. You know that feeling of desperately searching for the energy, time, and financial resources to bring your passions to life in the after-hour margins. You also wonder if you are following the right path, or when the doors will open for you. For years, I privately coined a phrase to capture this critical window of time for my pursuit of influence. I call it the "second shift." The second shift, as I mentioned in the preface of this book, is the span of time, after accounting for your primary responsibilities of the day, that you dedicate to directly or indirectly pursuing what really makes you tick—your dreams and passions.

> **The second shift is really a lifestyle—a way of being in relation to one's passion.**

On the surface, the second shift may just look like a particular time of day, or maybe even a season of life. But, that's only partially true. At its core, the second shift is really a lifestyle—a way of being in relation to one's passion. The second-shift lifestyle at its peak entails mastery of both chronology (the time one sets apart for passionate pursuits) and psychology (the mindset to drive its success). This is why, in fact, the second shift is our gateway to extraordinary influence. However, it often looks different for different people. Here are some of the most common second-shift pursuits to position one's passion for full-time influence:

- Part-time degree matriculation or training/vocational program
- Creating artistic expressions (e.g., books, films, music, blogs, sermons)
- Developing products (e.g., apps, crafts)
- Serving those in need (e.g., ministry, missions)

You may be a full-time homemaker whose first shift entails raising young children or homeschooling, but take night classes to finish your art degree. For you, the second shift is an educational door to realize your artistic aspirations.

Maybe you are like award-winning journalist Ivan Penn who, while excelling in a career with the Baltimore Sun, Miami Herald, Tampa Bay Times, and now Los Angeles Times, carves out time with his wife, September, to found a non-profit called the Power of Song, which is dedicated to educating youth and adults about the Civil Rights movement and social justice through song, theater, and art. For Ivan, the second shift is merging his affinity for music and culture to help people find life's meaning.

You may be like Jim, a young man I recently met who works full-time as a chemist for a major pharmaceutical company on the first shift, but works at the T-mobile retail store in the suburbs of a major metropolitan city on the weekends to get his "people fix" after dealing with geeky scientists all day. For Jim, the second shift allows his extroverted personality to flourish by serving customers.

You may be a physician, like Dr. Cynthia Warren, with a bustling pediatric practice in Philadelphia by day that satisfies her desire to heal children, but who works her multi-level marketing business on the second shift to promote financial independence for herself and others.

Maybe you are like New Jersey native Elliot Panzer, who works in the research field, programming surveys for pharmaceutical companies on his first shift to pay the bills. But, he gets his joy from strumming his guitar on evenings and weekends, performing local gigs with his band. For Elliot, the second shift is a time of right brain artistry that comes from a very different place than the technical demands of his first shift.

These are but a few examples of people making their dreams come alive on the second shift. In each case, the first shift serves an important function but it is the second shift that offers the fulfillment. Your second shift is not more or less important than your first shift. They each have a purpose. Do not allow anyone to discount the necessity or validity of your second shift. It is part of your formation process. Think of the second shift as a training ground of sorts for you to grow your part-time passion into its full potential to influence others' lives and bring you joy. Actually, I often think of my day job as providing the venture capital for my second shift.

Second-shifters are so inspiring because, for most of us, it is not the money and recognition that drive us. Rather, we are propelled by a visceral call and commitment to make a difference in the world, or to "leave a dent in the universe" as Apple co-founder Steve Jobs proclaimed.[7] Whether delivered through speech, pen, instrument, product, service, or accomplishment, we second-shifters have a message that cries out from within us to be told. It is a fire that must be fed. We all choose the extent to which we heed that call for influence. Sometimes, influence appears in unexpected ways.

Who were you created to influence? Take a few minutes and really think about it. For whom does your heart cry out? Whose pain do you feel? These are questions that almost always point you in the direction of your passion. Allow yourself to think broadly and outside the box. At home, it may be your spouse or

---

[7] Jobs, S. "Playboy Interview with Steve Jobs." Playboy, 1985.

partner or children. On your job, it may be a supervisor, peer, or customer. In your community, maybe it's your neighbor or even your barber. How would they describe your influence on them? The threads are practically innumerable if you allow your heart to guide you.

Influence, however, is never unidirectional. What I mean is this: you never influence someone without you yourself being influenced by that relational transaction. For example, I invited my barber, Sean, to breakfast to help him feel heard and to hopefully offer objective counsel regarding some family challenges he faced. The experience, however, also enriched me. Such is the nature of influence. We are created for influence — both the giving and receiving of it. Now that you have thought about who you influence, turn it around. Who influences you?

The reality is that influence is all around you. Think about it this way. Practically no one goes through his or her day without being influenced by someone. There may be no better gauge of the power of influence than renowned entrepreneur and motivational speaker Jim Rohn's instructive quote, "you are the average of the five people you spend the most time with."[8] Many years ago during my teen years, my wise grandmother, Minnie H. Penn, told me that she could tell the future just by looking at the people one hangs around. Who are the people that most influence you? For most of us, it includes the influence of friends, celebrities, and knowledge brokers through various media channels, whether traditional (e.g., television, radio, or print) or more contemporary (e.g., social media, podcasts, website) outlets.

How would you describe these individuals' influence on your life? For some of them, you see it as a positive experience

---

[8] Rohn, J. Facebook Official Jim Rohn. 2014 [cited 2015]; Available from:
https://www.facebook.com/OfficialJimRohn/posts/101545452305406 35.

that pushes you to be your best self. For others, it is a negative experience that causes stress and saps your life's vitality. With some, you experience both positive and negative influence. I have talked about influence as if it were always a positive force. We know that is not the case. That becomes a question of motivation — a topic which we will address in Chapter 3. For now, our goal is simply to appreciate that we all were created with threads of influence that connect us to others in mutually beneficial ways. That influence is imprinted in your DNA, and, until you accept that you are created for influence, you will struggle to hone in on your passion. But, find it you must, because passion is the engine that propels your influence.

PASSION: THE ENGINE OF INFLUENCE

Many people think about influence. Some of them even expend effort to convert imagined possibilities into actual results. But, few achieve their lofty aspirations. Why? It nearly always comes down to a question of passion — not whether or not you have passion (most people have some), but how much passion you have.

> **The depth of your passion fuels the breadth of your influence.**

People of extraordinary influence have deep, seemingly endless reservoirs of passion. Their passion consumes them. It is what they first think about when they wake up and the last thing when they retire for the evening. Passionate people are motivated towards influence because it is there that they most feel a sense of belonging. They know it as the space where they can fully express themselves — accepted for who they are rather than defined by a collection of brand-name clothes or fancy cars.

Passionate people want more life — the kind of life that prioritizes people over possessions. They see life's valleys as pathways to their next mountaintop experience, and mountain peaks as vistas to their true potential. Passionate people understand that real influence can only be fully grasped by seeing its intricate interconnection with their passion. Like fuel to a rocket, their passion is the energy that carries them from where they are to where they are destined to be.

Here is a simple way to think about it: The depth of your passion fuels the breadth of your influence. In other words, the number of people and nations ultimately reached by your message, compassion, products, or services is nearly always directly proportional to the sustained effort and enthusiasm that you dedicate to it. That is called commitment. Passion and influence are inseparable, and your influence is an external barometer of your passion's internal intensity. Influence, then, is simply the byproduct of your passionate action. More imagination and passion yield more influence. That is why, for me, Dan Miller nails it when he implies that passion is developed more than it is discovered.[9] As you discover your passion, you discover your influence.

This book is designed to empower you with the knowledge that allows your influence to flourish. To say that you are created for influence inevitably means that the sparks of passion (or maybe you think of it as "purpose" or "calling") have been within you for a long time. Years of positive and negative experiences have fanned the flames of your passions to where they are today.

Some may struggle to clearly hone in on where their passions lie, or to identify those whom they are supposed to influence. This is a real struggle for many who strongly desire to leave the world better than they found it. Some just don't know where to

---

[9] Miller, D., "'Passion' or just another shiny object?" in 48 Days. 2012.

start. Others struggle to sustain the momentum. If you sense the untapped power of your potential, be encouraged that this book's aim is to encourage you towards the passion and influence you are destined to have. You just have to imagine it.

CHAPTER 2

MASTER YOUR MARGIN

"Margin is the space between our load and our limits."

– DR. RICHARD SWENSON

The second shift has long been misunderstood. Too often, it has been assessed from a deficit perspective. We think to ourselves, When is second ever better than first? Would you choose second place over taking the first place prize? Would you prefer to bring the second product in a category to market, rather than being the pioneer who first broke the ground? Would you choose to need a second time around rather than getting it right the first time? For most people, the answer to these questions will generally be the same—a resounding "No." It seems to be an obvious answer, doesn't it? Usually, with the first position comes the reward and recognition. For us, first gives us a sense of pride and satisfaction. We—at least in Western culture—tend to be taught that second place is indeed "second class."

Many of us view our second shift as second rate. For years, that was me. I thought, If I was really talented, faithful, or courageous, I'd be a first shifter. I've long wondered how much better things would be if I was a first shifter. It is almost romanticized to think that life would be so much richer. I would be such a better person.

Conversely, as a second-shifter I feel disappointed and sometimes desperate, even though I know I am not alone. I listen to so many people who have come to loathe their first shift and consequently see their ability to pursue their passion on the first shift as a panacea. It feels like everything hinges on becoming a first-shifter.

When your passion is pursued part-time on the second shift, it can feel like your core essence is marginalized. You think you can only be true to yourself if you are a first-shifter — anything else feels like it is settling for less than your potential. You can get to the point where you almost literally feel like your day job is suffocating the life out of you. Often times, you even start to feel physically sick from the incessant strain of your day job. You feel like you are drowning, desperately hoping for something to come floating along that you can grab onto and ride out what feels like a psychological, emotional, and even relational whirlpool tossing you to the point of desperation. Believe me. I have been there. Sometimes, if I am completely honest, I still feel like I live there.

MY SECOND-SHIFT LIFE

I know a lot about the second shift. I have worked it my entire adult life. During my early 20s, my desire was to climb the corporate ladder in the Information Technology industry, in which I was employed. Going to graduate school full-time was not an option for me (being married with a young child and a healthy mortgage payment), but I wanted to acquire the technical skills that I believed would help chart my path. Accomplishing my goals required three and a half years matriculating part-time through a Systems Engineering graduate program.

As the years passed, my interests and passions began to shift away from the technology industry and towards helping enrich family life. This was a dramatic identity shift for me and required a very different knowledge base and skill set. This shift would inspire me to move my family across the country to pursue another graduate degree in Marriage and Family Therapy (MFT). I enjoyed this program tremendously, but it was immensely challenging, as I still had to work full-time while pursing my degree. In addition, this time, the degree could only be pursued on a full-time basis. So, for three years, I worked full-time (still in the Information Technology arena) and went to school full-time too. For two of these three years, I also had to separately perform practicum-training hours as part of my MFT degree requirements.

Those were tough years. I knew, however, by this time that one of my passions was to help families—and I had developed the mindset and determination that failure was not an option. I had moved my family three thousand miles, from one coast to another, in pursuit of a dream. I not only had to finish, I had to finish well. Little did I know then that this mindset would be essential to my next steps.

After completing my MFT degree, I moved my family back across the country again to enroll in a psychology doctorate program. This full-time program provided me a small living stipend; however, students were not allowed to work outside of the program. In some ways, this was a welcome relief for me—given my pace of the prior three years. In addition to a little more free time, it gave me an opportunity to put many of the relationship skills I had acquired to practical utility, volunteering in a faith-based setting. So, while my day "job" was now as a full-time doctoral student and employee of the university, my second shift entailed coordinating a lay counseling program for a large church in Philadelphia, as well as serving as one of the counselors.

After completing my doctorate, I began a career in market research, leveraging the research and analytic skills that I had acquired during my doctoral education. However, with a passion to impact family life, I accepted a larger second-shift volunteer role at my local church, taking on the role of Director of Christian Education in which eleven church ministries and dozens of ministry volunteers reported to me. With a demanding full-time market research job, my second-shift mindset and drive again had to become quite focused over the four-year span in which I maintained both of these roles.

After deciding to write my first book, *Marriage ROCKS for Christian Couples,* I knew it was again time for me to transition my second-shift activities from serving the church to founding my own organization (Discovering Family International), developing books and other resources, securing speaking engagements, and marketing these products and services. Today, my second-shift initiatives have become even more focused as I produce weekly blog posts and podcasts to add value to those interested in my voice.

I hope for the day when I can pursue my passion on the first shift without jeopardizing my family's lifestyle—but that day is not yet here. And, realistically, I don't know when it will be. That has personally been the source of much anxiety. However, over the past seven years, my angst has led to greater understanding of the second shift and finding creative ways to generate that attitude that positions me for full-time influence.

For the majority of us second shifters, our day job is not our passion. It is our obligation—a means to care for our responsibilities and those dependent on us. That is noble. But, so often it leaves us feeling unfulfilled. You may get some sense of satisfaction from these endeavors . . . but, deep within, we know that we were created for more. The reality, however, is that the second shift is not second-class to the first shift. There are at least five legitimate reasons why you may not yet be in a position to pursue your dreams on the first shift:

- Current work/school/ministry obligations require a full-time commitment
- Financial status of the family would be compromised
- Important family relationships would be strained
- Enjoyment of your role and responsibilities
- Passions and dreams are not yet well-defined

One or more of these concerns may be a temporary obstacle to becoming a first shifter. But, none of them are acceptable excuses to not pursue your dreams or do what my friend Dr. Daniel Lee calls "doing what you're built for."[10] Doing what you are built for is your task, regardless of the shift on which you do it. The first and second shifts serve an equivalent purpose. That purpose is to develop you as a VIP.

LIVE LIKE A VIP

We commonly use the acronym "VIP" to mean Very Important Person, with access to special privileges, status, or importance. Celebrities, heads of state, corporate executives of major companies, and financially wealthy individuals command VIP status at the places they frequent. Our social structures are designed to acknowledge and accommodate their status as distinct from the average Joe or Jane.

Have you ever been tagged a VIP at a function you've attended? Maybe it was a front row seat at a concert or an exclusive table at a select function. Maybe it was traveling first class on an airline flight. As someone who frequently speaks in front of audiences, I am often graced with this VIP designation. It feels nice to receive special attention and service. In fact,

---

[10] Lee, D. & Anderson, F., *Do What You're Built For: A Self Development Guide Using Coaching Principles*. 2008: AuthorHouse.

sometimes we even pay extra money to experience that VIP treatment.

I would like to borrow this VIP term to highlight a different group of people—those who are also select and special, but for a different reason. For us, VIP means Vocational In Passion. Let me break that down to really give a clear sense of its intent. First, let us examine the word vocation. Today, we use the word to refer to a profession that could be secular or sacred. We use it primarily to speak generically about what one spends their time doing—typically what one does on the first shift. However, the word vocation derives from the Latin word *vocationem*, meaning "calling" in a spiritual sense. Prior to the 16th century, one would have used the word vocation to refer primarily to the "call" by God to an individual. I like the way it is represented by Wikipedia: "The idea of vocation is central to the Christian belief that God has created each person with gifts and talents oriented toward specific purposes and a way of life."[11] St. Paul captures this idea in the Book of 1 Corinthians, saying, "Let each one remain in the same calling wherein he was called" (7:20, NKJV). To say it another way, you were born into your vocation or your calling. It is your birthright. Your life is then spent bringing your vocation into physical manifestation. We will address that more deeply later in this chapter.

Now let's contemplate the second part of the VIP phrase, vocational in passion. By appending 'in passion' to vocational, we intently address the idea that the grand work of our lives—or our divine purpose, if you will—is fueled by the passions within us. Your passions are not random. They are by design. The Creator gave you these passions as a birthright for a specific purpose. As you yield to that purpose, you are a VIP.

---

[11] Wikipedia, "Vocation." Available from:
https://en.wikipedia.org/wiki/Vocation

You can see that being a VIP has nothing to do with whether you are a first or second shifter. Being a VIP is not about how much money you amass in doing what you enjoy. Being a VIP is not about celebrity and fame. And, as Pastor Andy Stanley so deftly described during the 2015 Catalyst One Day conference, being a VIP is not about pursing the myth of autonomy — that belief that you do not have to answer to anyone.[12] Whether you are a VIP on the first or second shift, you are accountable to someone. Your pursuit of influence on the second shift makes you a VIP of equal standing with someone doing the same on the first shift. As a VIP, the expanse of your influence is just as meaningful on the second shift as the first shift. I hope this encourages you that your shift is not an indication of success or failure. VIPs, regardless of their current shift, are by definition successful because they are deliberately following their divine calling with intentionality.

When listening to the success stories that proliferate on the Internet and other platforms, one can easily become fixated on the excitement of having a lifestyle business (a business that conforms to the needs of your life flow and demands), of making six- and seven-figure incomes, and having that illusive freedom. These are appealing benefits to many of us, and they are indeed very possible for you. The reality, however, is that whether you are a first- or second-shifter, becoming a VIP takes a lot of work to maximize your potential. It takes systematic and long-term commitment to invest in your knowledge, manage your resources (including your time and money), and grow your relationships. There are no shortcuts.

Unfortunately, as in so many other areas of our lives, we look for that mythical shortcut anyway. We think about the Very Important Persons of our culture and think there is a side

---

[12] Stanley, A., Andy Stanley Leadership Podcast, in The Dangers of Autonomy. 2015.

entrance to avoid waiting in the long line. We think there is the phone call that pushes our need to the front of the queue. We think there is the connection that gets us a free pass. It is, by and large, a farce. There are no back doors to becoming a VIP. Similarly, there are no bypasses to the first shift. Yes, without a doubt, you have access to fulfill your VIP potential and even to become a first-shifter, if that is your desire. But, like the automobile driver looking to take the busy freeway to her destination, everyone has to take the on-ramp to get access. To stay with the analogy, there are express lanes on the highway to allow you to get to your destination faster. Some of you will leverage the abundant resources (like this book) to accelerate your pace. Others will stay in the far right lane and move more slowly. But, regardless of your chosen lane, you still have to take the journey to fully develop who you are as a person and exponentially expand your territory.

In Day Job to Dream Job, author Kary Oberbrunner captures this idea with excellence in stating that we do not discover our dream job until we become the person worthy of it.[13] Using Oberbrunner's idea, whether your desire is to become a first-shifter or to maximize your second-shift influence, you have to go through the process of becoming a VIP.

So, I have now demonstrated that it is not the pursuit of one's purpose that differentiates the first and second shift. You can become a VIP on both of them. So, what is the difference? It's margin. Second-shift VIPs, by necessity, become masters of life's margins. That is what sets us apart.

THE MARGIN WALKERS

Merriam-Webster's dictionary describes margin as "an extra amount of something (such as time or space) that can be used if

---

[13] Oberbrunner, K., *Day Job to Dream Job: Practical Steps for Turning Your Passion into a Full-Time Gig.* 2014: Baker Books.

it is needed."[14] Understanding the second-shift lifestyle requires a clear understanding of margin. When people think about margin, they almost always think exclusively about time. While time is one type of margin, there are also others.

Our goal is to consider four types of margin that collectively characterize our human experience. These are chronological, psychological, physiological, and financial margins. Those margins, or what you may think of as your true discretionary resources after your fixed obligations are addressed, are different for each of us. Richard Swenson, in his excellent book, *Margin: Restoring Emotional, Physical, Financial, and Time Reserves to Overloaded Lives,* defines margin as the space that once existed between our lives and our limits.[15] He proceeds to offer a compelling admonition to better monitor how we are increasingly using that margin to merely survive. I really appreciate this vantage point. Yes, we must be healthy in managing our margin. But, the reality is that we second shifters rely on that margin. It really is not an option if we are to live like VIPs.

Though we often focus on the time margin, all four of these are equally important to maintain a balanced quality of life. Too much sacrifice within any of them for an extended period of time will jeopardize your well-being and your relationships with those who care about you. For most people in current society, life has some degree of margin.

1. Time Margin

After accounting for the time commitments of your day and essential life responsibilities, there is some time left—hopefully.

[14] Merriam-Webster. "Margin." Available from: http://www.merriam-webster.com/dictionary/margin.
[15] Richard A. Swenson, M., *Margin: Restoring Emotional, Physical, Financial, and Time Reserves to Overloaded Lives.* 1995: NavPress.

The amount of remaining time is your time margin. Do you have an accurate sense of how many hours actually make up your time margin? Many people do not, because they do not deliberately account for their time. While I do so pretty diligently now, it has not always been that way—particularly during my young adult years. After finishing my undergraduate degree, starting my first professional job at IBM, and being newly married, I really thought I had little time margin for anything else. I felt like I was tapped out. If, at that time, you had asked me how much time margin I had, I would have balked and suggested maybe a few minutes in a given day. Then, something remarkable happened.

My church issued a 30-day challenge for the laity to go through a time of consecration in which we were to abstain from television watching, Internet surfing, and video games, and implement some dietary restrictions. At the time, I was not concerned about the dietary adjustments, but I was flabbergasted by the suggestion to give up television for an entire month. That seemed unreasonable. Actually, I considered simply not doing that part of the challenge because it felt so extreme.

Much of my discretionary time then centered around television, movies, and, to a lesser extent, video games. At that time, I actually had the habit of walking in from work and turning on the television. It was always on, even if it was just background noise while I attended to something else. The television stayed on until it was time for me to go to bed five or six hours later.

Ultimately, I decided that I would fully abstain from television watching for the thirty days. It was very hard. I felt like I went through a withdrawal process somewhat akin to a mild case of what a drug or alcohol addict might endure. I missed my shows a lot at first. But, as time went on, that pull decreased. By the end of the thirty days, my eyes were opened. I was profoundly struck by something that never before occurred to me — the opportunity cost of television watching. I did not realize that, by spending so much time watching television, I was not productively seeking to understand my designed impact and pursue other things. By cutting down only my television time, I gained hours of discretionary time every day. My faulty perceptions of time margin were adjusted. I then had several hours each night to use productively to do more reading and writing.

> **Time is such a precious commodity that you must deftly guard with vigor, but give with favor.**

Pursuing your own ultimate VIP status on the second shift requires a continual assessment of your time margin. Time is such a precious commodity that you must deftly guard with vigor, but give with favor. This balance is hard. It starts with an honest assessment of which time commitments in your life are really fixed and which are optional. Usually, fixed time commitments include a job, child-rearing responsibilities, volunteer commitments, and basic daily activities such as eating and sleeping. Most other activities are discretionary. How much can you multiply your time margin by cutting back on things that are not directly contributing to your pursuit of influence? If you are like most of us, you can save several hours a day by halving your television viewing and your time on the Internet (including Facebook and other social media sites). We will return to this point in more detail later. The key to grasp is that you may not be optimizing your time margin, and that compromises your ability to optimize your second shift success.

2. Psychological Margin

Though time tends to be the first margin we think of, it is far from the only critical aspect to second shift success. Another important facet is psychological margin. Psychological margin refers to the mental and emotional acuity that one still has after dealing with the personal, vocational, relational obligations, and stressors of the day. As with time, many factors impinge upon your psychological margin. It could be factors that you face on a daily basis, such as the nature of the work that you do on your first shift or the age of your children. It could be concern about future events such as rumored layoffs or stress about a presentation you have to make next month. It could be driven by your high achieving or procrastinating personality. All of these factors and more influence your baseline mental capacity.

After dealing with these exigencies, you still have to face your second-shift commitments. What you have left in reserves is really driven by what you started with in the first place. I can use my wife and myself as fairly extreme examples of different psychological margin baselines. I am a high-energy person who is driven by the accomplishment of goals. Even after a long day on my first shift, I have mental energy and fortitude to go for several hours non-stop on the second shift. My wife is different. She is an introvert, and really prefers to have her down time in which she can allow her mind to rejuvenate. After dealing with her day job, she most enjoys going to her Zumba dance or weight conditioning classes to give her mind time off.

The other component here is one's emotional intelligence. Emotional intelligence is understood as the ability to identify, use, understand, and manage emotions in positive ways to relieve stress, communicate effectively, empathize with others, overcome challenges, and defuse conflict. Of course, higher emotional intelligence better positions you with psychological margin, because you are better able to deflect life's inevitable stressors from negatively affecting you as much as they otherwise might. The result is that you have more psychological margin for your second-shift engagement. Whether mental or emotional capacity, it is not a matter of right or wrong—it is simply knowing what your capacity is, in order to maximize them as you pursue your second shift. In some cases, you may need to get some third-party help from a therapist, pastor, or trusted friend to help process your stressors in order to free your mind for your second shift. Of course, at times, you may need to slow down on your second-shift pursuits in order to give your mind a break. This is something you have to constantly monitor, because if you have a mental breakdown you are not being of service to yourself or anyone else.

The final component of psychological margin is relational. Your relationships impact your mental health. If you are married, the vitality of your marriage directly impacts your psychological margin. A strong and supportive marriage is going to create more margin for you, while a frustrating and critical one erodes your margin. Healthy relationships with your children, extended family, friends, and trusted others have this same empowering or disempowering element. Second shifters who operate at their full potential intuitively understand that building healthy relationships with those closest to them offers the reward of increased margin that can be dedicated to their second-shift pursuits.

3. Physiological Margin

Our physical bodies have limitations. While those limitations vary from person to person, we all have boundaries beyond which we cannot push ourselves. The question, however, is how much physiological margin you have left for your second shift. Physiological margin is driven by your health status. Chronic illnesses—such as diabetes and high blood pressure—take a toll on your body. Others must handle even more difficult illnesses and pain. It is difficult to focus on the second shift when your body is wracked with pain. A person in good health is simply going to have better physiological margin than someone who has to manage multiple health conditions. Therefore, it is important to work to maintain a healthy lifestyle. Eat healthier foods. Establish a consistent fitness routine. Lose weight, if necessary. I am a runner, and while I don't always particularly enjoy running, I do enjoy the health benefits.

The other physiological factor is the physical strain that your day job places on your body. If you have a job that entails a lot of manual labor or other physically demanding activities, these will impact your margin. Do what it takes to preserve, or even increase, your physiological margin.

4. Financial Margin

The final aspect of margin to address is financial in nature. Much of our lives revolves around the accumulation and expenditure of money. Unfortunately, too many Americans are over-leveraged and in difficult situations with credit card debt and other unsecured debts, as well as mortgages that they are barely able to pay. When you are in a financial crisis, it causes tremendous strain on you personally—and on your family as well. This lack of financial margin makes it very difficult to focus on growing your second-shift influence. Conversely, if you have been a smart money manager, after accounting for the financial obligations of your lifestyle, there are some economic resources left. This is your financial margin.

While successfully growing a platform does not have to be expensive, it does have its price. There are monthly and annual costs of doing business. For example, I pay fifteen dollars a month for audio hosting for my podcast. I pay another fifteen dollars monthly for Mailchimp—my email distribution service—

and I pay a number of other expenses for memberships and courses to learn how to better grow my business and influence. I am able to handle these expenses because my wife and I have financial margin. Without that financial margin, one has to responsibly avoid incurring additional expenses. That, of course, slows down your movement up the second-shift learning curve.

FIVE TIPS FOR MASTERING YOUR MARGIN

When viewed collectively, it should be clear that life's stressors constrain the bandwidth that you need to optimize your second-shift influence. Second shifters who are most successful are margin walkers. A margin walker is someone who creates, preserves, and leverages life's margins to truly be vocational in passion. In this way, they model practices for others to follow. That is called leadership. Sustaining this marathon, however, requires an attentiveness to make timely course corrections that prevent you from burnout and allow you to think long-term.

Scripture offers a poignant example of a life-saving mid-course correction in the book of Exodus as Moses approaches physical and psychological exhaustion serving as a judge for the Hebrew nation (Exodus 18). His father-in-law, Jethro, notices a disturbing pattern and asks Moses directly, "Why do you sit alone, and all the people stand around you from morning till evening?" (verse 14). Moses responds, "Because the people come to me to inquire of God. When they have a dispute, it comes to me, and I decide between one person and another, and I make them know the statutes of God and his laws" (verses 15-16). Moses sees his work as God-centered, just as you and I do. But, his inability to create margin has taken its toll. Jethro aptly responds, "What you are doing is not good. You and the people with you will certainly wear yourselves out, for the thing is too heavy for you. You are not able to do it alone" (verses 17-18).

The message is clear. Life without margin mastery hurts you and the people that you are called to serve. Even your well-intended efforts may be suboptimal, because you refuse to listen to those God puts in your path to help you master your margin and correct your course.

Here are five process improvement tips that you can start putting into practice this week, which will help you to develop margin mastery over the long haul.

- **Tip #1:** Awaken thirty minutes earlier each day this week and commit that cumulative 3.5 hours to your VIP process.
- **Tip #2:** Randomly tell three people who are important to you why you appreciate them.
- **Tip #3:** Eliminate one thing from your diet this week that you know is bad for your health.
- **Tip #4:** Allocate 1% of your income this week to a personal development course.
- **Tip #5:** Identify an accountability partner to ensure that you complete these five tips.

Mastering your margin is a daily decision to do something small that makes a big difference. As Darren Hardy implies in his book, The *Compound Effect: Jumpstart Your Income, Your Life, Your Success,* it is little everyday decisions that will either take you to the life you desire or to disaster by default.[16] Each day, there are barriers and resistance to wielding influence on the first and second shift. We second shifters have to leverage the compound effect to reach our dreams. We have the necessary attitudinal, time management, and relational acumen to move ahead. But, let's be realistic. There are different challenges to

---

[16] Hardy, D., *The Compound Effect: Jumpstart Your Income, Your Life, Your Success.* 2012: Vanguard Press.

follow that vocational passion on the second shift as compared to the first. Managing the challenges of the second shift requires second shifters to embody the determination and persistence to push through the barriers and master the margin necessary to gain and sustain your platform of influence. Later chapters of the book will offer invaluable guidance to discern how to use your margin to change others' lives and, in the process, transform your own.

CHAPTER 3

GODPRINT: THE DNA OF INFLUENCE

"We ask to know the will of God without guessing that His will is written into our very beings."

– ELIZABETH O'CONNER

Sometimes, you just want to know that someone hears you. You want to know that you matter. Though it often feels elusive, you know that you were created for influence. But, you want that deep sense of satisfaction that your voice makes a difference. At your lowest points, you wonder why you keep pushing yourself. You sometimes question, though too tepidly to speak it aloud, "Would anyone even notice if I stopped?" Those are the difficult days. It's the doubt that gets you.

Yes, the doubts. They are legion—like demons. They possess you and, like the rhythm of a carousel, circle round and round in your mind. The doubt demons, however, do not operate alone. They are but a catalyst for a larger evil that is known by many names. In his bestselling book, The War of Art, Steven Pressfield calls it "the Resistance."[17] In the Holy Bible, the Apostle Peter coins the term "Adversary" (1 Peter 5:8). Here we refer to this axis of evil as the DRAGONS (Doubts, Regrets, Apathy, Greed,

---

[17] Pressfield, S., *The War of Art: Break Through the Blocks and Win Your Inner Creative Battles.* 2012: Black Irish Entertainment LLC. pg. 7.

Obstinance, Narcissism, and Scarcity). We will thoroughly examine the DRAGONS in later chapters.

For now, just know that the DRAGONS make you question who you are, what you do, and even why you do it. Similar to the lore around these mythical fire-breathing creatures, DRAGONS conjure fear, destruction, and bondage. DRAGONS are good at their job, leaving no stone unturned. They magnify your fears, undermine your self-confidence, destabilize your relationships, and shake your faith. Armed with an arsenal of lies (their tool of choice), the DRAGONS pursue a singular purpose—to diminish, if not completely destroy, the ultimate influence for which you were created. While we all face them, they seem particularly pernicious to those of us on the second shift.

The DRAGONS tell you that your dreams are too big for you. When you try to generate some positive direction, the DRAGONS make you question whether you will ever have enough time to do it right. By keeping you focused on your visible resources, the DRAGONS leave you feeling that you will never accrue the financial or relational capital to maximize your potential. The DRAGONS paralyze you by keeping you focused on your own egotistical needs, rather than the more abstract question of why you exist. The DRAGONS tell you that you're too old, too young, too late, too poor, too inexperienced, too ugly, too tired, and too busy. The DRAGONS feed on shame that, in her book, Daring Greatly, Dr. Brene Brown calls "the intensely painful feeling or experience of believing that we are flawed and therefore unworthy of love and belonging."[18] Extending her thought, she describes shame as the universal fear of disconnection being brought on by our failure to live up to some ideal or goal, and thus unworthy of connection.

Alex Sclamberg, co-founder of Elevate Gen Y and dubbed "the self-help voice of her generation," offers compelling caution

---

[18] Brown, B., *Daring Greatly: How the Courage to Be Vulnerable Transforms the Way We Live, Love, Parent, and Lead.* 2015: Avery. pg. 68.

about the DRAGONS in the 2012 Huffington Post article, "The Real Reason You're Not Living Your Dream Life." She writes, "They're not truths; they're only as real as you make them. They're artificial creations that mask the real fear and doubt lurking underneath your skin."[19] She is right. Even when others encourage you that the DRAGONS' lies are baseless, you dismiss it as platitudes. You question how you can convince your family and those closest to you to believe in your dream, when you even struggle to see how all of the pieces fit together. Such is the DRAGONS' debilitating fire. The DRAGONS want you to accept the lie that your dream is too big for you to pursue on the second shift.

But, there is good news. While the DRAGONS have power, they do not have power over you. You need not be afraid of their fire. With the truth in hand you, my friend, are fireproof. Yes, we all get singed at times by the DRAGONS' heat. But, rest assured, it will not consume you. Stay encouraged and resist the DRAGONS' lies, because your second-shift preparation is someone's miracle.

A SECOND-SHIFT MIRACLE

For me, Joey and Rajni's story begins like many others that I see—with a marriage in crisis. When I first met this newlywed couple, their marriage was already on the verge of collapse. They were off to a rocky start, to say the least. I first met them at a two-day marriage retreat that my wife Dalia and I were conducting in Williamsburg, Virginia for a military unit out of Fort Meade, Maryland. Joey and Rajni asked to meet with us privately during a lengthy afternoon break. The crisis was

---

[19] Sclamberg, A., "The Real Reason You're Not Living Your Dream Life (And It's Not Time or Money)." 2012 [cited 2015]; Available from: http://www.huffingtonpost.com/alexis-sclamberg/dream-life_b_1820160.html.

immediately clear. Though married only a few months, they were emotionally strained. Rajni was particularly unsure that the marriage would work. Joey seemed oblivious as to how to make her happy. They were both at their wit's end. I couldn't help thinking to myself, "How did such a young couple become so desperate in such a short amount of time?" But, I so appreciated their courage to seek help.

Dalia and I felt as if we were able to make modest progress during our short time with Joey and Rajni at the retreat. I hoped we had made a difference. It wasn't until a few months later, however, that I received a disturbing Facebook message from Joey. Things had deteriorated. I could feel the helplessness in Joey's words. His love for his wife was clear. But, he was losing her. Did he have what it would take to save his marriage? I wasn't sure. But, I believed in Joey and Rajni. Despite the uncertainty that swirled around them, there was something about them that made me believe. My goal was to give them the hope that I had for their marriage. Joey and I exchanged message after message to encourage him to win his wife back. Things seemed to be improving. Then, the messages stopped.

On my birthday of that year, I received a message from Joey that in many ways is the inspiration for this book. Though I lamented having to be out of town for work on my birthday, I received this message that changed everything.

Dr. Harold. First, I want to tell you Happy Birthday. Today my son was born. It wasn't a coincidence that God chose today. You were the saving grace of my marriage. I will never forget the help you have given me. I can't wait until he is older so I can tell him about you. We will have this special day to remind us of you for many years to come.

I could not stop smiling. For a few moments, I forgot about my day job and its frustrations. I forgot about myself. A tear formed in the corner of my eye. A precious child was born on that very day (my birthday) because a marriage was saved. I was created to help Joey, Rajni, and their son. The threads of our lives intersected and formed something beautiful. That day, the DRAGONS were quiet. It was a miraculous reminder that I was created for extraordinary influence—all of which happened on the second shift.

GODPRINT: THE DNA OF INFLUENCE

Imagine a world where Michael Jackson never recorded an album, Michael Jordan never played basketball, and Michael Flatley never danced. Just for a few moments, close your eyes and imagine that they were never even born. Our world—certainly the musical, basketball, and dancing aspects of it—would be a very different place. Other than having the same first name and each using his feet to international acclaim, these three men had one other thing in common: influence through innovation. They each changed "the game."

Michael Jackson "influenced everyone who came after him," according to Steve Greenberg of S-Curve Records.[20] With the array of singing sensations like Usher, Justin Timberlake, Chris Brown, and countless others crediting Jackson's influence, there is probably very little hyperbole in Greenberg's assertion, certainly among pop music artists.

Or, how about Michael Jordan, about whom 13-year NBA veteran and Hall of Fame inductee, Gary Payton, says, "we all became better players because of who he was and what he did. He raised everyone's talent. He raised the stakes. He elevated the

---

[20] France, L. R., "'King of Pop' was major influence on younger artists." 2009 [cited 2015]; Available from: http://www.cnn.com/2009/SHOWBIZ/Music/06/25/jackson.young. artists/index.html?iref=24hours.

game."[21] Even today, every basketball superstar is measured again Michael Jordan. And, to this day, every one has fallen short.

In 1994, American-born Irish dancer, Michael Flatley, broke with Irish dancing tradition at the annual Eurovision event. In what was subsequently dubbed the "seven minutes that shook the world," he catapulted Irish dancing from a regional affair to the international spotlight in the dance sensation that became Riverdance. Hence was born the "Flatley revolution" that changed the landscape of Irish dance and even claimed a couple of Guinness World records in the process for both the most taps in a second (35) in 1998 and highest paid dancer at $1.6M per week in 1999.[22]

Few would contest the global influence of the three Michaels. Their accomplishments and accolades are legendary. Whether glove-clad moonwalking like Jackson, dunking from a foul line takeoff like Jordan, or breaking the arm position tradition of Irish dance like Flatley, the Michaels' creativity catapulted them from celebrity to superstar status.

Here, however, is the kicker. Your influence and purpose are just as important as theirs. It is easy to dismiss my assertion as preposterous. They are, after all, internationally recognized. Their estates are worth millions of dollars (even posthumously in the case of Michael Jackson). In some ways, they seem untouchable. All of this is true. But, it misses a critical point. The Michaels innovated what they were created to do. In that way, your call is no different.

---

[21] Powell, S., "Jordan's Lasting Legacy." 2013 [cited 2015]; Available from: http://www.sportsonearth.com/article/41714646/.
[22] Flatley, M., Available from:
http://www.michaelflatleyireland.com/rd.htm.

> **Creativity is in your DNA. Successful living is innovating WHY you were created.**

Some find it difficult to equate their pursuit of influence with that of the Michael's. One of the reasons is a limited understanding of creativity.

We tend to think of creative people as painters, poets, sculptors, musicians, and similar artisans. Creativity, however, is much more expansive. Consider this definition of the term. Creativity is "the ability to transcend traditional ideas, rules, patterns, relationships, or the like, and to create meaningful new ideas, forms, methods, and interpretations."[23] In other words, you are creative when you meaningfully change the status quo.

I've coined the term "GODprint" to refer to your unique WHY. GODprint is the unique manifestation of the Creator in you. When you work to change the status quo, you, the created, become the creator (with a little c). Your innovation reflects a partnership of sorts (co-creation) with the Creator (with a big C). You were created to create. In this way, you co-create with the Creator.

Like the fingerprint which forensic science uses to identify your physical body, your GODprint distinguishes your unique purpose. As a confluence of your personality, proficiency, and passions, your GODprint represents your call—the altruistic purpose for which you were created. If we break down GODprint, the G is for gifts. These are the talents and skills at which you are good. The O in GODprint represents the opposition that you face which shapes who you are as a person. Opposition is important to your becoming process. Think, for

---

[23] Dictionary.com, "Creativity." Available from
http://dictionary.reference.com/browse/creativity

example, about your opposing thumbs. Without them, try to pick up a penny off the table or to button your shirt. It is practically impossible. Opposition is essential to who you become. The D in GODprint is for direction. Direction is the specific path that God has for you to journey. Your path encompasses your experiences. Your path determines the way that you interpret and narrate the things that you have experienced. Your path is the series of places at different points in time that your presence is integral to the outcome that God has for you.

Author and Trinity Forum co-founder, Dr. Os Guinness, defines calling this way: "calling means that our lives are so lived as a summons of Christ that the expression of our personalities and the exercise of our spiritual gifts and natural talents are given direction and power precisely because they are not done for themselves, our families, our businesses or even humankind but for the Lord, who will hold us accountable for them."[24]

Your GODprint is your calling because it informs your voice. And, your voice is literally (and figuratively) your mouthpiece to the world. When reflecting your GODprint, your voice is the unique sound through which your creativity is expressed. And, because it originates from a transcendent source, it always strives to serve a transcendent purpose.

Influence is the byproduct of a commitment to the pursuit of your GODprint. Though we tend to wish it were different, you will not ultimately control the outcome of your pursuit of influence. That is in the hands of providence. It has to be that way because the Creator sees the bigger picture—things far beyond our understanding.

---

[24] Guiness, O., *The Call: Finding and Fulfilling the Central Purpose of Your Life*. 2003: Thomas Nelson.

> **Your highest calling is obedience to
> your GODprint.**

What you control is your obedience and commitment to the pursuit. In doing so, you have equaled (if not exceeded) the Michaels. At the end of your life, you will have lived your best life. You have made the best of the hand that you were dealt. Whether that transforms one family (like Joey and Rajni) or millions (like the Michaels) is actually immaterial. Your highest calling is obedience to your GODprint.

There is an excellent biblical parable (The Parable of the Talents) found in Matthew 25 that illustrates this responsibility. In this parable, a master entrusts three servants with varying amounts of resources to invest for him. To one he gives five talents (biblical currency), to another two talents, and to the third he gives one talent. The master then departs the region for a lengthy period of time. The servants who received five and two talents invested what was entrusted to their care and were able to provide a 100% return to the master. However, the servant with only one talent did nothing with what was placed in his care. He simply gave the master back what was originally given to him. While the savvy servants were handsomely rewarded by the master, the lowly servant was called slothful, lazy, and was ultimately deposed by the master.

This is a well-known parable that has been extensively used to talk about stewardship. But, while writing this book, God showed me a perspective on this parable that I had never before seen. The passage reads as follows: "To one he gave five talents, to another two, to another one, <u>to each according to his ability.</u> Then he went away" (Matthew 25:15, emphasis added). The master dispensed those talents according to what he already understood as the ability of each servant. Most interpret this parable to suggest the servant receiving five talents had the most ability. Conversely, the one receiving the one talent had the least ability. We are not exactly told the nature of these abilities. But, it is clear that there was a difference. Yet, what is also clear is that the master expected the servant of the least ability to still produce. Less ability, less talent, less resourcefulness, or less intelligence were not acceptable excuses. The master believed that even the least-skilled servant had the requisite ability for success.

Your GODprint is the Creator's investment in you. He has bequeathed you with the personality, proficiency, passion, and path to reap a magnificent harvest. But, the message is clear. Your responsibility (and mine) is to provide a return on the Master's investment, rather than squandering the opportunity. Your ability has nothing to do with God's expectations. That may seem harsh, but I'm convinced that this is God's way of telling us that we cannot rely simply on our own abilities. We have to tap into His abilities and His grace.

Where is your GODprint directing you? The Apostle Paul touches on GODprint in his own way, noting, "We have different gifts, according to the grace given us. If a man's gift is prophesying, let him use it in proportion to his faith. If it is serving, let him serve; if it is teaching, let him teach; if it is encouraging, let him encourage; if it is contributing to the needs of others, let him give generously; if it is leadership, let him govern diligently; if it is showing mercy, let him do it cheerfully" (Romans 12:5-8, NIV).

In Chapter 1, I outlined the reason it is critically important to start with your WHY as you build the foundation of your platform. Its higher order origin, and your conviction to it, makes your WHY the catalyst for extraordinary influence for organizations and individuals like you and me. Your WHY serves a transcendent purpose.

This book presents a framework (the HOW) that will guide you in growing your part-time passion to extraordinary influence. But, if you do not first start with your WHY, your efforts will fall far short of your potential.

Stephen Covey, author of the international bestseller, *7 Habits of Highly Successful People*, writes in this classic's sequel, *The 8th Habit: Moving from Effectiveness to Greatness,* "The crucial challenge of our world today is this: to find our voice and inspire others to find theirs."[25] As in the Parable of the Talents, Covey captures the multiplicative impact of following one's GODprint. When one walks in his GODprint, it is measured by its benefit to others.

Civil rights leader and Nobel Peace Prize laureate, Dr. Martin Luther King, Jr. chides the DRAGONS and eloquently promotes GODprint in an excerpt from a 1957 speech, "An individual has not started living fully until they can rise above the narrow confines of individualistic concerns to the broader concerns of humanity."[26] Covey and Dr. King got it right. Your GODprint is your ally against the DRAGONS because it shifts your attention away from simply serving your own egotistical needs to embracing relational authenticity.

Regardless of your ethnicity, gender, or social status, you are destined to make a difference that matters. Don't get me wrong; everyone will not have an impact that matters. But, you will. In fact, you are probably reading this book because, despite a litany of challenging people and circumstances, you already sense your power to choose that path of influence. Unlike others who may content themselves with the status quo or being "good enough," something inside you constantly yearns for more. But, the question is, more what?

That question is an important one. Actually, it is the question that everything hinges upon. It forms the line dividing two types

---

[25] Covey, S., *The 8th Habit: From Effectiveness to Greatness.* 2013: Simon and Schuster.
[26] King, Jr., M. L., Dr., Conquering Self-Centeredness. 1957: Montgomery, Alabama.

of influence seekers. Your GODprint is always directed towards that which is positive and shedding light into dark places. It must be so because that is the heart of the Creator. However, each of us is left with free will. We choose whether our GODprint will indeed move people in a positive or a negative direction. Like the biblical parable of the talents, some will invest their talent to multiply its impact on the world. Others, more interested in self-preservation, will bury their GODprint and ultimately deprive us of their extraordinary influence.

To illustrate the difference in how people choose to use their GODprint's influence, let's look at the insect family for clues. I associate these different groups with two types of insects, the bees and the fleas, with whom they metaphorically share distinguishable characteristics.

THE BEES

Our insect friends, the bees, are flying insects. There are more than 20,000 known species of bees — the most famous being the honeybee. Bees can be found on every continent except Antarctica. Bees are most notably recognized for their role in pollination — transporting seeds from one plant to another. Bees' role in fertilization and reproduction is critical to the ecosystem.

You are reading this book because that bee symbolizes your desired impact within your own ecosystem. This book is written for you, the bee. Bees, like you, seek to fertilize the lives of others by cultivating more empathy and compassion to truly feel like they can identify with those in need. Through education, mentoring, and other forms of empowerment, bees seek to reproduce themselves. Some seek more knowledge to cognitively understand and help with the challenges people face. Still others desire more resources to provide economic and social supports to the impoverished and those in dire financial straits. Bees pollinate influence to wield extraordinary success.

As of this writing, I live in the Philadelphia metropolitan area. When I think of a historical example of the bee, Benjamin Franklin first comes to mind. Some have called him "the First American." As symbolized by the bee, this renowned polymath's "pollination" is legendary. He used his gifts as an author, printer, political theorist, politician, postmaster, scientist, inventor, activist, statesman, and diplomat to clearly elevate himself as one of America's most influential Founding Fathers.

THE FLEAS

The fleas, however, are a different story. Fleas are wingless, blood-sucking insects. They do not fly. Relative to their body size, they are among the most capable jumpers of all known animals. They jump onto a host with a single intention—to feed off of the host's blood. Their bodies are tough, making them able to remain affixed to their host when exposed to extreme pressure. The flea feeds on the blood of the host, as much blood as fifteen times their body weight, which allows them to reproduce.

Unfortunately, their human counterparts are similar. Yes, these human fleas also seek influence. But, it is a self-serving dark side of influence. The fleas desire more influence in order to satisfy their egotistical needs. They see life as self-centric, with everything and everyone else simply existing for their own pleasure.

The flea succumbs to what John Ortberg dubs the "Shadow Mission" in his insightful book, *Overcoming Your Shadow Mission.*[27] The shadow mission is a degeneration of the heart that robs you of your calling and leaves in its place deep soul dissatisfaction. If you are a flea, you may have influence. But, it is negative energy that will ultimately destroy you.

---

[27] Ortberg, J., *Overcoming Your Shadow Mission*. 2008: Zondervan. pg. 2.

To make this a little clearer, I offer an example of an historical influencer that I would classify as a flea: Adolph Hitler.

Yes, he had extraordinary influence. As a decorated World War I veteran, he eventually rose to power by attacking the Treaty of Versailles and promoting pro-German sentiment. But, this influence was at the expense of Jews, Blacks, and anyone that did not fit his Arian ideal. His charismatic appeal and political deftness elevated him to German Chancellor in 1933, when he sought to position his Third Reich to establish a New Order. Ultimately, Hitler's shadow mission costs the world millions of lives, generations of hurt, and, of course, his own soul. There are probably few better examples of the blood-sucking flea than Adolph Hitler.

If you are an unapologetic flea, let me save you some time. Unless you are willing to change your motivations, this is the wrong book for you.

WHICH INSECT ARE YOU?

Admittedly, using Benjamin Franklin and Adolph Hitler to contrast the bee influencers from their flea opposites is extreme. Our daily lives are replete with much more modest examples.

Adam Braun, American businessman, author of New York Times bestseller, Pencils of Promise, used his intelligence and compassion to found Pencils of Promise, a non-profit organization that builds schools and increases access to education for children in the developing world. Adam Braun is a bee.

Brilliant physicist Steven Hawking, former Lucasian Professor of Mathematics at the University of Cambridge and author of A Brief History of Time, which was an international bestseller, uses his GODprint to try and disprove God's existence. I appreciate his intelligence. But, I'm saddened by his choice. Hawking has said, "When people ask me if a god created the universe, I tell them that the question itself makes no sense … We are each free to believe what we want, and it's my view that the simplest explanation is; there is no god. No one created our universe, and no one directs our fate. This leads me to a profound realization; There is probably no heaven, and no afterlife either."[28] I believe that Stephen Hawking has sullied the community of science away from its Creator. By no stretch of the imagination do I equate his choices with those of Hitler. But, to my mind, Stephen Hawking's quote represents a flea mindset that may outweigh his inner bee.

The key point to grasp is the role of motivation. Each of us must consider our own motivations as we go about our daily routine. In the 2012 movie Stand Up Guys, Al Pacino (whose character name is Val) presents a stark example of the bee and flea within each of us as he seeks absolution from the priest during confession. The somewhat crude exchange goes like this:

Val: "Forgive me, Father, for I have sinned."

Priest: "How long since your last confession?"

Val: "60 years, give or take a few."

Priest: "Now, confess each and every serious sin that separates you from Christ."

Val: "Oh no, we'd be here forever. Why don't we just deal with today? So far, I shot a guy in the kneecap and one in the arm. I stole a bunch of prescription drugs and a sweet-a** car. I

---

[28] Hawking, S.; [cited 2015] Available from:
https://www.goodreads.com/quotes/551152-when-people-ask-me-if-a-god-created-the-universe.

punched a Korean store clerk in the face and took his clothes. And, I had sex with a hooker four times."

Val: "But I did some good things too, Father. I buried a friend. I helped this young woman take her life back. And, I eased my best friend's pain. So can I say a Hail Mary and be done here?"

Priest: "I don't think you can Hail Mary your way out of this one."

Val: "You're right."[29]

The question is not whether we are 100% bee or flea. Though an extreme depiction, we—like Pacino's character, Val—are both. We all have seeds of good and evil within us. Author J. K. Rowling writes in Harry Potter and the Order of the Phoenix, "We've all got both light and dark inside. What matters is the part we choose to act on. That's who we really are."[30] The Holy Bible expresses the same point in Luke 6:45, "The good person out of the good treasure of his heart produces good, and the evil person out of his evil treasure produces evil, for out of the abundance of the heart his mouth speaks."

Remember these three truisms to help maintain focus:

- The one (bee or flea) that you feed is the one that grows.
- You can never prioritize the giftedness (talents/abilities) evident in your GODprint over the character (virtues) demanded the Creator.

---

[29] Stevens, F., Stand Up Guys. 2013. pg. 95.
[30] Rowling, J. K., *Harry Potter and the Order of the Phoenix*. 2004: Scholastic.

- The greater your giftedness, the heavier the burden placed on your character. Without sufficient character, your giftedness will crush you.

Always leverage your bee nature over your flea tendencies. The bee must reflect the abundance of your heart. That is the part that you choose to act upon. There is a Zen Buddhist saying that says, "how you do anything is how you do everything."[31] Will your inner bee define you, or will you allow your flea's parasitic tendencies to dominate your life? My prayer is for the ultimate expression of your bee, because only that can truly capture the possibilities of your GODprint. Feed your bee by vigilantly monitoring your interactions with others, looking for opportunities to pollinate them, and suppressing those tendencies towards selfishness.

---

[31] Huber, C., *How You Do Anything Is How You Do Everything: A Workbook.* 1988: Keep It Simple Books.

CHAPTER 4

KNOW YOUR WHY

"The place God calls you to is the place where your deep gladness and the world's deep hunger meet."

— FREDERICK BUECHNER

DISCERN YOUR GODPRINT

When I was a doctoral student, one of my professors sought to ease our collective anxiety about choosing a topic for one's dissertation. The dissertation is the defining process for a Ph.D. student, and is a hurdle that stumbles many doctoral students. It has to be an original body of research. In other words, you have to find some topic that has never been researched before and find it interesting enough to spend several years of your life becoming an expert on it. With all of the anxiety of this dissertation process ahead of us, the professor assured us that we should not worry about finding our dissertation topic. He assured us that if we kept reading, our topic would in time find us. It probably comes as no surprise to you that this was not reassuring to me at all. Frankly, it felt like hogwash. I wanted a process—steps to follow. I did not feel like I had forever to figure this out. I wanted to be pointed in the "right" direction. Needless to say, I was on my own. But, you know what? He was exactly right. I just kept reading. Some things were interesting to me; other things were not at all. In a matter of months, I saw my dissertation topic as plain as day. Eureka! I chose Transformational Leadership Among People of African Descent. It would become the largest quantitative research of African American leadership ever conducted. It was hard work, and I am quite proud of it.

Related to your GODprint, there is one key point I would like you to glean from this dissertation story: Your GODprint is not something that anyone can dictate to you. Your specific GODprint is not in any self-help book. That can be frustrating, and even upsetting, when things do not seem to develop at the pace you would like. We often wish it was as easy at that. I am a preacher's kid who, in my teen and young adult years, was frequently told that I would be a preacher like my father. Well, now that I am a midlife adult, I am pretty confident that this is not true. No one could predict my GODprint or tell me how to discover it.

> **Your GODprint will find you, if you are available and listening.**

I believe that you will ultimately find the pinnacle of your GODprint at the intersection of your internal wiring (DNA) and your environmental experiences—many of which will be out of your control. While no one can tell you your GODprint, there are ten signs that—like the clues in a mystery thriller—direct you to know when you are journeying in your GODprint.

1. Hours feel like minutes when you are in the flow
2. You feel more alive than ever
3. You never seem to be able to get enough of it

4. You would do it for free

5. You enjoy the company of others with this same interest

6. Your creativity is at its peak

7. Trusted others validate your abilities in this area

8. You dream (day/night) about it

9. You take steps to become the best you can possibly be at it

10. The lives of others are enriched by your efforts

So, how do you discern your GODprint? You follow your heart. You listen to wise and trusted friends. You seek Divine inspiration. You act. When you continue to pursue this, you will eventually find that place where all ten of those GODprint signs are evident. I tell you this with the same unequivocal confidence that my doctoral professor told me. Your GODprint will find you, if you are available and listening.

Recently, I decided to increase my level of engagement in my barber's life. For several years, I have engaged in thirty-minute conversations with my barber, Sean, as he cut my hair. Sean's life and mine never intersected outside the barbershop. Sean, who is quite a few years my junior, was going through some challenging life circumstances. Our life journeys are very different, but I feel a connection to this young man. There is something magnetic about him. So, I decided to invite him out to breakfast. He accepted, and we had a very nice time connecting—allowing those threads to intertwine more deeply. I like the Ancient Chinese proverb, "when the student is ready, the teacher will appear." Here's the irony: Was I Sean's teacher or was he mine? The answer, of course, is "both." When you are ready, your GODprint will be clear. But, it will always be discovered in the action you take. The well-known interaction between Mother Teresa and ethicist John Kavanaugh is the best depiction, I believe, of the way one's GODprint is discovered.

When John Kavanaugh, the noted and famous ethicist, went to Calcutta, he was seeking Mother Teresa . . . and more. He went for three months to work at "the house of the dying" to find out how best he could spend the rest of his life.

When he met Mother Teresa, he asked her to pray for him. "What do you want me to pray for?" she replied. He then uttered the request he had carried thousands of miles: "Clarity. Pray that I have clarity."

"No," Mother Teresa answered, "I will not do that." When he asked her why, she said, "Clarity is the last thing you are clinging to and must let go of." When Kavanaugh said that she always seemed to have clarity, the very kind of clarity he was looking for, Mother Teresa laughed and said: "I have never had clarity; what I have always had is trust. So I will pray that you trust God."[32]

Trust. This is what my professor had expected of me as well. Rather than focusing on clearly discerning your GODprint, just trust God and follow the call of your heart. Then, you will spend the rest of your life clarifying its call as it evolves.

THE CREATIVITY OF GODPRINT

As earlier noted, when you are operating in your GODprint you are partnering with the Creator to co-create something that positively impacts humanity. You are innovating beyond the status quo. I am of the belief that our GODprint leads us down one (sometimes more) of four paths, through which you have extraordinary influence. In the classic book, *My Utmost for His Highest*, author Oswald Chambers says, "Your creative mind is the greatest gift God has given you and it ought to be devoted entirely to Him."[33]

---

[32]Berry, C., "Jesuit Philosopher Recounts Time with Mother Teresa." [cited 2015] Available from:
http://www.catholiceducation.org/en/faith-and-character/faith-and-character/jesuit-philosopher-recounts-time-with-mother-teresa.html.
[33] Chambers, O., *My Utmost for His Highest*. 2010: Discovery House.

> **Untapped potential leaves you feeling unfulfilled and confused at best; and at worst, disillusioned and betrayed.**

The world needs your unique GODprint. If that feels like hyperbole to you, then I am glad that you are reading this book, because it is far from extreme. Be careful not to discount the importance of your influence. Many selfishly think that no one is harmed but themselves if they do not pursue their calling. The reality is much starker. Psychologist Carl Jung captures it best in saying, "Nothing has a stronger influence psychologically on their environment and especially on their children than the unlived life of the parent."[34] How can that be?

Imagine someone giving you the keys to a brand-new Lamborghini Veneno Roadster. At a starting price of $4.5 million, this 750-horsepower, 12-cylinder car can go from 0-62 mph in less than three seconds. This Italian auto has a top speed of 221 mph. That is one fast (and expensive) ride. With the keys in hand, you get behind the wheel and start the ignition. As the engine jumps to life, you feel the power at your command. Your heart is racing. You feel invigorated just thinking about how extraordinary the vehicle is. The pictures didn't do it justice. This is truly a masterpiece of engineering and design that oozes luxury. And, for this moment it beckons to your command. As you shift the transmission into drive and slowly maneuver to the open highway, you realize that this is a probably a once-in-a-lifetime experience for you. You want to test what this baby can really do. Is it really as remarkable as touted? But, as badly as you want to really experience its power, you worry what might happen if you go too fast. It's too dangerous. You may lose

---

[34] Jung, C., [cited 2015]; Available from:
http://www.quotationspage.com/quotes/Carl_Jung.

control. Your mind fills with all of the negative things that could happen. So, you decide to play it safe, never going about 70 mph — the maximum speed that you've driven before in your Toyota Camry. After an hour of driving around, it's time to turn the keys back in. You pull back into the lot and slowly emerge from the vehicle. While the experience was unique for sure, you feel disappointed. Yes, you can tell everyone that you drove the Lamborghini Roadster. But, you know that you did not really experience it. A life unlived is going through the motions of life well beneath your potential. Yes. Technically, you lived. But, really you did not. Whether behind the wheel of an exclusive Lamborghini or steering the decisions in your own life, untapped potential leaves you feeling unfulfilled and confused at best; and at worst, disillusioned and betrayed.

Jung's assertion is correct. If your life is lived below your potential, the ensuing shame has far-reaching consequences — especially on those closest to you. You take out your frustration on those that matter most to you. The energy that you spend wrestling with your own DRAGONS keeps you from connecting with and investing in those who depend on you. The skepticism and jaded belief system that has stunted your progress becomes the straitjacket that constrains the progress of your children, friends, co-workers, teammates, and partners. The result is almost always emotional distancing from the very people you were created to serve.

Reaching your true potential only happens as your own DRAGONS are tamed. That is your call. Nothing less. So many dreams languish in a cacophony of good intentions. Good intentions are practically meaningless. DRAGONS bent on your destruction could not care less about your good intentions. As Andy Stanley, senior pastor of Northpoint — an Atlanta mega-church — posits, it is one's direction not one's intention that determines one destination. He calls this the "Principle of the path."[35] The well-known proverb says it a little differently (though connoting the same message), "the road to hell is paved with good intentions." As Andy Stanley portrays, taming your DRAGONS and actively directing your future all depend on what direction you are facing. Are you facing the direction of your dreams or your DRAGONS?

Contrary to what you might expect, you do not slay your DRAGONS by facing them. Let us consider the mythological story of the muses to understand. In Greek mythology there is a story of the muses. The muses lure you with their enchanting sound. Unknowingly, sailors—entranced by the muses' melodic incantations—realized too late that they had been directed off course into their death. Like the muses, the DRAGONS want you distracted and attending to them, rather than facing the direction of your dreams. Do not misunderstand me . . . I do not mean to suggest that we bury our heads in the sand and deny the DRAGONS' existence. The DRAGONS are real. Their attack is real. What I am advocating is that you do not let them divert your attention from your dreams. Keep your eyes on the prize. That proverbial prize is your ascent to the position of influence for which you were created.

START WITH WHY

Throughout the pages of this book, we will examine many tactical steps in this journey. The truth, however, is that successfully facing your destiny—despite the DRAGONS' fire—requires an understanding of what Simon Sinek, in his New York Times bestseller, *Start with Why: How Great Leaders Inspire*

---

[35] Stanley, A., *The Principle of the Path: How to Get from Where You Are to Where You Want to Be*. 2011: Thomas Nelson.

Everyone to Take Action, calls "The Golden Circle."[36] The Golden Circle is comprised of three concentric circles, each inside the other. These three circles represent your WHAT (outer circle), HOW (middle circle), and WHY (inner circle).

Your WHAT represents what you present to others. For a company, it is the products and services they sell. Even if you are not explicitly producing conventional products or services, you are always "selling" your ideas, aspirations, and beliefs. Would-be leaders often err, however, in prioritizing their WHAT over everything else. Though sometimes getting short-term success, it is often fleeting because it fails to tap into an emotional core. As Sinek explains, there is a biological reason for this. The WHAT is processed through the part of the brain called the neocortex (the "newest" portion in our brain's evolution). The neocortex is rational, analytical, and has the capacity for language. In other words, your WHAT helps people cognitively understand what you offer. It is important in building your influence. But, we all know that understanding is not usually the primary driver of behavior. You will not wield extraordinary influence by starting with your WHAT.

The middle ring in the Golden Circle is your HOW. This is your method or steps that you take to position yourself as a person of influence. The HOW is critical because it is the conduit through which your uniqueness converts to influence. These are the steps that you take to live extraordinarily. Much of this book is about the HOW—an influence-generating engine called the "second shift" developed expressly for those like you who are committed to having extraordinary influence in spite of major limitations on your time and resources. We will return to a fuller description of the second shift in later chapters because this HOW is also not your starting point.

---

[36] Sinek, S., *Start with Why: How Great Leaders Inspire Everyone to Take Action.* 2009: Portfolio. pg. 37.

The Golden Circle's innermost ring is our starting point. This is your WHY. Your WHY is what makes you distinct from everyone else. Unlike the WHAT that is rooted in your brain's neocortex, your WHY emanates from the oldest, most powerful portion of your brain called the limbic system. It is your emotional core that allows you to tap into the emotions of others. These corporate examples may help grasp the centrality of the WHY. Apple makes computers, tablets, and music players (WHAT). But, as Sinek outlines, Apple's co-founders, Steve Jobs and Steve Wozniak, understood Apple's WHY as allowing the little guy to take on the corporation. This noble WHY has driven decades of unsurpassed innovation.

Harley Davidson is another example. Harley Davidson's WHAT is motorcycles. We all know that. But, Harley Davidson's WHY is more about lifestyle. People do not buy a Harley just to have a good motorcycle. Consumers purchase a Harley Davidson to make a statement about who they are.

Apple and Harley Davidson are examples of lifestyle brands. A lifestyle brand is a brand that attempts to embody the interests, attitudes, and opinions of a group or a culture. WHY unites people because it represents a shared perspective—a rallying point. Your WHY defines your tribe and provides the emotional capital to influence. Our goal is to establish your WHY as a lifestyle brand for those waiting to hear your message. I call this WHY your GODprint because, like the fingerprint, it uniquely differentiates you from everyone else. GODprint acknowledges the transcendent origin and purpose of your WHY. As your personal mission statement, your WHY serves as your intrinsic motivation to make the world a better place.

Our culture needs more DRAGONS slayers. With a clear WHY and a commitment to HOW, you have everything you need to slay your DRAGONS and, as importantly, to develop products, services, and relationships (the WHAT) that empower others to defeat their DRAGONS as well.

This book was written to arm you with the tools to succeed in this battle for your territory—the expanse of your influence. Throughout the chapters of this book, you will not be content to just resist the DRAGONS. You will attack them blow by blow, like the woodsman's axe to a tree, until they are permanently disabled once and for all. Through the grueling and glorious process, you will become a much different person than you are today. That, after all, is the point. You will become the person worthy of your dream.

Over the years, it has become clearer why I was created. I was created for the mother and son that I described in this book's preface, who were enriched by a blog post. I was created for Joey and Rajni—and their son—whose marital trajectory was impacted by a workshop. I was created for my barber, Sean, over thirty-minute stents in the barber chair. And, of course, I was created for you. But, it all started with me knowing WHY I am here and pursuing that with a spirit of excellence.

The quote by Frederick Buechner at the beginning of this chapter is one of my all-time favorites, as it points squarely to the "WHY question" that lies within each of us. He says, "The place God calls you to is the place where your deep gladness and the world's deep hunger meet."[37] How do you start with WHY? It is leaning into your own deep gladness with intentionality and purpose. It is knowing that your WHY is about way more than just yourself. It is sensing the deep hunger that consumes those around us. So many people are longing for someone to care about them without attempting to impose an agenda on them. You are their answer. You were created for them. They are your WHY. That's where you start. As Mother Teresa said, it isn't about clarity. It's about trust.

---

[37] Buechner, F., *Wishful Thinking: A Theological ABC.* 1973.

PART 2:

THE ATTITUDE OF INFLUENCE

CHAPTER 5

THE ATTITUDE OF INFLUENCE

"Everything can be taken from a man but one thing: the last of human freedoms—to choose one's attitude in any given set of circumstances, to choose one's own way."

—VIKTOR FRANKL

Now that you have a sense of the direction of your GODprint, we must focus on the single factor that will most determine your success in your pursuit of influence. Fortunately, as Viktor Frankl suggests above, that factor is the one thing over which you actually have total control—attitude. Attitude is everything. Frankl's storied history certainly speaks to the incredible power of having the right attitude. Viktor Frankl—an Austrian neurologist, psychiatrist, and Holocaust survivor— spent several years working with the mental health needs of fellow prisoners at Auschwitz and other concentration camps. Frankl believed that what motivates people is a "striving to find meaning in one's life."[38] That drive for meaning, he concludes, is

---

[38] Frankl, V., *Man's Search for Meaning*. 4th ed. 2000: Beacon Press. pg. 104.

what carries them through and helps them to overcome painful life experiences. Frankl's hypotheses were honed under the most de-humanizing of conditions. But, I believe that they also speak volumes for the course of most of our lives. Whether done constructively or destructively, we all search for meaning. The issue, however, is that so many people are searching for meaning in other people, places, and things. That ultimately amounts to futile meandering.

I recently sat down with a young man in his twenties who was frustrated, despite a strong internal desire to make a difference in the world. He is clearly searching for that meaning that Frankl describes. But, his frustration with his lack of clarity and feeling of being stuck has led him to engage in some negative behaviors in his life that are affecting him and his new wife. Unless his search emanates from and remains consistent with his GODprint, he could spend years, and even decades, in futility. It is only when we commit to an attitude to "Pass I On" that we really find that true sense of identity and meaning. When we look at the etymology of the word influence, we can see why it is so intricately linked to the concept of "Pass I On." The word *influence* comes from the Medieval Latin term *influentem*, meaning "to flow into." Influence is literally allowing your passion to flow into others. In other words, the search for meaning has to first begin within, and then extend outward.

> An attitude of influence flows from within you into a reservoir that is bigger than you.

Sometimes the search stays centered in the home, in the successful raising of children and a healthy home life. Other times, that search extends out into service in the community. And, sometimes, there is a search to impact lives across the globe. There is no right answer for everyone; there is only a best answer for you. Regardless of its target, an attitude of influence flows from within you into a reservoir that is bigger than you.

If I can adjust the famous Vince Lombardi quote about winning,[39] I might say, "Attitude isn't everything. It is the only thing." Attitude is a psychological and emotional commitment to a belief. Having an attitude of influence first requires you to believe that you are such a person. If you do not first believe in yourself, it is very difficult for others to believe in you. In the midst of life's stressors, you still have the privilege to choose how you react. In a real sense, life is not about what happens to you. Most of the time, you simply cannot control this. Life is about how you choose to react to what happens to you. The attitude of influence is to choose to believe in your GODprint, regardless of what circumstances bring.

In her book, *Mindset: The New Psychology of Success,* Dr. Carol Dweck presents two contrasting mindsets that characterize our human experience. One she calls the growth mindset, which is "based on the belief that your basic qualities are things you can cultivate through effort."[40] When operating from a growth mindset, the individual "believes that their true potential is unknown (and unknowable)" because of the inability to gauge the ultimate impact of their passion, skills, and relationships. A person with a growth mindset might say to themselves, "the sky is the limit," because they trust their GODprint to present boundless opportunities for personal growth and influence.

In contrast, Dr. Dweck argues that those with a fixed mindset believe that their qualities and opportunities are essentially set in stone. She suggests then that these individuals feel an urgency to prove themselves over and over. A person with a fixed mindset might be heard saying, "I'm just playing with the cards I was

[39] Lombardi, V., [cited 2015]; Available from:
http://www.vincelombardi.com/quotes.html.
[40] Dweck, C., *Mindset: The New Psychology of Success.* 2007: Random House. pg. 7.

80

dealt." You can almost feel the implied resignation. Things simply are what they are. They do not see that attitude is a choice, as Frankl suggests. When operating from a fixed mindset, people appear threatening and options seem limited. She writes of those with this fixed mindset: "if you have only a certain amount of intelligence, a certain personality, and a certain moral character—well, then you'd better prove that you have a healthy dose of them."[41]

This distinction between the growth and fixed mindset is critical to your second shift success. Those with the growth mindset see the second shift as a passionate place that allows them to creatively explore that which most interests them. A growth mindset allows the second shifter to leverage the resources in the margin to incrementally increase the impact they have. The fixed mindset, however, sees the second shift from a "glass half empty" perspective. They lament what they do not have and become mired in negativity and self-limiting beliefs.

Second-shift mastery only happens with a growth mindset. Can you have some successes with a fixed mindset? Yes. You can, but you will always live short of the influence that you were created to have. And, there are forces at work in the universe to ensure that this stunted life is exactly what happens to you. These are the DRAGONS. Their job is to keep you in a fixed mindset at all costs—feeding your mind with a barrage of reasons why you cannot follow the leading of your GODprint. I must say, they are a pretty convincing foe.

Over the next several chapters, I will continue to explore the DRAGONS extensively, because I believe that awareness of the way they work is the key to defeating them. But, fortunately, we also have an advocate who pushes us to remain true to our purpose to grow personally and relationally. I call this attitude

---

[41] Ibid, pg. 6

the "KINGDOM" mindset (Knowledge, Insight, Novelty, Grace, Deference, Other-centered, and Much). We will dig into each KINGDOM aspect in later chapters as well. For each of the DRAGONS, there is a KINGDOM response to affirm who you are and sustain your attitude of influence. In the following chapters, we will examine the psychological, spiritual, and relational warfare between the DRAGONS and the KINGDOM for control of your thoughts.

CHAPTER 6

THE DRAGONS' SHADOWLANDS

"My attitude is that if you push me towards something that you think is a weakness, then I will turn that perceived weakness into a strength."

— MICHAEL JORDAN

Though the DRAGONS are no laughing matter, I must admit that I chuckle sometimes as I think of them. They remind me of a childhood memory of a DC Comics cartoon that I used to watch called Super Friends, that included such superheroes as Superman, Wonder Woman, Aquaman, and others. They were part of the Justice League. Of course, the Super Friends faced archvillains — collectively called the Legion of Doom — led by Lex Luthor, the infamous enemy of Superman. Here is how Lex Luthor described the Legion of Doom's mission: "It is the purpose of the legion to align our infamous forces against the powers of good and defeat them, leaving us the rulers of the world."[42] You have to give it to Lex Luthor. The Legion of Doom's mission statement was clear.

Every time I think of the DRAGONS, I think of the Legion of Doom's ominous mission statement. The DRAGONS (doubt,

---

[42] Urbano, R. P. C., Wanted: The Superfriends. 1978.

regret, apathy, guilt, obstinance, narcissism, and scarcity) align their insidious intentions to disrupt your GODprint by promoting your inner flea and suppressing the power of your bee. The DRAGONS want control. I want to be clear on this point. The DRAGONS recognize your skills and passions. In fact, they count on them. The problem, however, is that the DRAGONS seek to divert your attention from the positive intentions of your GODprint to the shadow mission that was earlier described.

> When you are operating in your authentic GODprint, your mission is about honoring the Creator and serving people.

The DRAGONS' domain is the shadowlands. They desire for you to spend as much time there as possible—until you can no longer distinguish them from reality. The DRAGONS want the shadowlands to become what you identify as normal. When that happens, your GODprint is lost. Let me explain . . .

Your shadow mission is so dangerous because the DRAGONS make it feel like you are in your wheelhouse—doing exactly what you are meant to do. Your shadow mission has many of the signals of your GODprint . . . but it's a lie. When pursuing your shadow mission, your thoughts and actions are ultimately based on your selfish desires. Conversely, when you are operating in your authentic GODprint, your mission is about honoring the Creator and serving people. Your authentic GODprint encourages your relationships as an expression of God's unique design for you. But, your shadow mission encourages relationships to give you a sense of significance or worth. The shadow mission feeds your ego and, in doing so, feeds the DRAGONS. When you feed the DRAGONS, a predictable thing happens. They grow larger. The larger they grow, the more they distort your GODprint.

Your shadow mission is not why you were created. It is only a reflection—a shadow. Your shadow mission serves you. Left unrestrained, the DRAGONS will ultimately transform you from a designer's original into a copycat who tries to emulate others rather than creating a fresh path. Unless you are very careful and tuned in to your authentic self, sometimes the subtlety between your true mission and your shadow mission can be difficult to discern.

To demonstrate this subtlety, let me use my own example. Here is my mission: "Give the Christian and broader faith community tools to pursue authentic and meaningful relationships through the systematic integration of godly principles." This mission statement captures the "builder" nature of my GODprint with the "systematic integration." It also highlights the tendency of my voice to orient towards people of faith—though I contend my message transcends the faith community. It demonstrates my passion for relationship building, and it grounds my perspective in what I deem as evergreen (timeless) principles.

For comparison's sake, now I present my shadow mission: "To achieve international recognition and material success as an authority and creative thinker on relationship-building paradigms." Closely compare my mission and my shadow mission. Can you see the elements common to both? Both capture my passion for relationship building. Both acknowledge creativity and thinking outside the box. In other words, both reflect the "builder" nature of my GODprint. When I have compared my mission and shadow mission in workshops, I inevitably have several people in the audience who see nothing wrong with my shadow mission. In fact, some like it. That is exactly what makes it so dangerous. It feels right. It feels like it nails your GODprint. I can look at my shadow mission and see its aspirational quality. It feels like success. But, where does my shadow mission go awry?

My shadow mission taps into my achievement drive and strokes my ego with the pursuit of acclaim and material success. If I follow that shadow mission, I will ultimately lose everything that really matters. Could I achieve international acclaim by listening to the DRAGONS? Possibly yes. But, at what cost? You will only find ultimate joy by doing what you were created to do. It is not riches. It is not the number of Facebook friends or Twitter followers or the size of your email distribution list. It is not the number of speaking invitations that you receive or the size of your bank account. You need simply look at how many miserable people have all of those things to know that this true. Celebrities, who ought to be on top of the world, are dying from drug overdoses as they try to escape the pain of living. Many wealthy people struggle to enjoy the fruit of their labor because all they can do is labor. Yet, the DRAGONS keep pushing them—making them feel as if they have no options.

I am focusing on the DRAGONS so that you can recognize the cunningness of their dark arts. With knowledge, you can fight them. They never go away completely—even when you suppress them for a season, as you become more successful, they will try to rise again. That is to be expected. Actually, it is a signal that you are on the right track. It is bad news when you no longer feel the DRAGONS' presence. That means one thing— they have consumed you.

> The power of your GODprint, when you follow its path, is always greater than that of the DRAGONS.

But, when you are fighting the DRAGONS, that means that they see you as a threat. You are making a difference. You are pursuing your GODprint. You are seeking extraordinary influence. The DRAGONS are out to stop you. The good news is that the power of your GODprint, when you follow its path, is always greater than that of the DRAGONS. You will always defeat them if you stay out of the shadowlands.

Here, I will expand details about the DRAGONS and, in the next chapter, equip you with the method to defeat them with a KINGDOM mindset (Knowledge, Insight, Novelty, Grace, Deference, Other-centered, and Much).

Your true prize and the promise of your GODprint lies in the KINGDOM.

DOUBT: THE HEAD OF THE DRAGONS

Doubt is the catalyst—the "point man" for the DRAGONS. Doubt, the first component of the DRAGONS, is responsible for planting the destructive seeds that can set the full negative cascade in motion. The danger of doubt is two-fold. First, it is by definition a state of limbo. It is neither belief nor unbelief. It is something in between. And, "in between" can be a dangerous place. Second, doubt can be a good thing when it incites hesitation to fully consider one's response. In other words, doubt can result in prudent and cautious waiting periods. Most often, we look at that as a good thing. Sometimes, that doubt will keep you away from things that are potentially harmful to you as you rationalize why you really should not be taking a certain unwise action. In those moments, doubt is your ally.

However, doubt can also generate unbridled procrastination and indecision. Doubt can render you functionless—paralyzed indecision. That is not a good thing. Try a simple experiment. Turn your head (but not your torso) as far to one side as possible. Then try to walk straight ahead in the direction your torso is pointing. It's nearly impossible to walk straight. The problem is that where your head goes, your body follows. You will lose your way. And, the longer it continues, the more you risk losing your very soul.

The DRAGONS count on doubt to keep you off-balance. At its most basic, doubt is characterized by uncertainty and questioning. As such, it interrupts the two related ingredients that are most critical to your pursuit of influence. By definition, doubt is the antithesis of trust and belief. Yet, trust and belief are essential components of faith. When you put the pieces together, doubt and faith cannot coexist. They are like darkness and light. Doubt, like darkness, dissipates in the presence of faith's light.

The DRAGONS want you to doubt your purpose, passions, value, and vision. To accomplish this feat, doubt reminds you of your failures, shame, insecurities, fears, and anything else that will cause you to hesitate about mobilizing your GODprint. Doubt will leave you feeling like your influence is marginalized and that your fears are center stage. When aligned with the DRAGONS, doubt engenders self-doubt. It whispers in your ear a lie that sounds something like this: "There is no way you can achieve your dream. That's a fantasy. You don't have what it takes." When doubt seeks to interrupt or contradict your GODprint, you know that it is the DRAGONS' work.

THE POWER OF KNOWLEDGE

Most of our human systems are built on a basic paradigm: "seeing is believing." This mantra has, in fact, been the cornerstone of the modern philosophical thought. It is scientific and rational. If something can be seen or observed, then we have to acknowledge its existence.

However, embracing the fullness of your GODprint cannot be understood with this modern lens. You have to believe what is inside you before you can convert it into action. Your belief in your GODprint is the necessary catalyst for you and others to experience its impact. The more you believe is there inside you, the more you will see is there. Of course, the converse is true as well. The less you believe is inside you, the less that you will demonstrate. It is a self-fulfilling prophecy.

The DRAGONS use uncertainty and self-doubt to paralyze your movement towards influence. At some level, there is always doubt. The antithesis of doubt is knowledge. Knowledge, the first aspect of the KINGDOM mindset, is your ally against doubt's cascade of self-limiting beliefs. However, knowledge does not necessarily mean that you have a clear answer to a material question. Rather, knowledge means that you retain a clear awareness of your own self-worth and clear faith in what you were created to become. Maintaining your knowledge that you serve a critical role in other's lives best marginalizes doubt's influence. It is how you slay the head of the DRAGONS. When doubt is curtailed, the DRAGONS go mysteriously silent—at least for a season.

REGRET: THE DRAGONS' COMPASS

To be human is to have a past. No one is pleased with everything from one's past. Things happened—good and bad. Mistakes were made. And, it is this aspect of our human nature upon which regret feeds. Regret is a negative emotional state that involves blaming ourselves for a bad outcome, feeling a sense of loss or sorrow about what might have been, or wishing we could undo a previous choice that we made.

Regret serves as the compass for the DRAGONS. Just like a true compass always points north, regret always points to the past. But, not in a fair and unbiased way— regret pinpoints the mistakes and missed opportunities. Regret ruminates and feeds on your disappointments while marginalizing the good that you have done. The DRAGONS' strategic use of regret is simple. Regret keeps you looking backwards, so that you can never follow your dreams forward or heed your GODprint's call.

89

The reality is that most of us can readily identify some past error of commission or omission that we wish we could do over. That is a natural and understandable desire. Regret, however, becomes dysfunctional when it convinces you that your past mistakes demonstrate that you are "all bad," rather than being a good person who made a mistake. Regret wants you to feel that you are a mistake by replaying your past errors across the canvas of your mind as proof.

Regret may start with mild disappointment. If allowed to fester, it morphs into deep-seated depression, disillusionment, and detachment from your passions. The negative impact, however, is not just psychological. Regret impairs your physical well-being as well. According to Psychology Today, "Research, reported in the AARP Newsletter, shows regret can result in chronic stress, negatively affecting hormonal and immune system functioning. Regret impedes the ability to recover from stressful life events by extending their emotional reach for months, years, or lifetimes."[43] Regret seeks to ensure that your past becomes your peril.

REDEMPTION: THE FORERUNNER OF INSIGHT

While regret seeks to constantly pull you back to past missteps and hurts, forgiveness loosens regret's distended grip. Forgiveness is not denial. It acknowledges past errors. But, forgiveness strips these incidents of their power to cripple you.

Forgiveness has many layers. For some, forgiveness means releasing yourself from the guilt of one's past. For others, forgiveness means moving beyond the pain that external parties have caused you. Forgiveness is a divine proposition, in that it taps into attributes of the Creator (such as grace and mercy) in

---

[43] Greenberg, M., P. D., The Psychology of Regret. 2012 [cited 2015]; Available from: https://www.psychologytoday.com/blog/the-mindful-self-express/201205/the-psychology-regret.

your GODprint. The redemption story is always a narrative of how God uses the highs and lows of your life's testimony to heal yourself and others. Redemption means the releasing of a debt.

In a tangible sense, forgiveness transforms regret to redemption. This is a powerful conversion experience because the cleansing power of redemption washes away the stench of regret. Forgiveness shifts your focus from looking behind you to looking up to God—even (and maybe especially) when your emotions are wounded.

Dr. Neal Roese, professor at Northwestern University's Kellogg School of Management and a leader in the field of regret research, has conducted many studies on the science of regret. Interestingly, his studies have shown that regret is actually considered by most people to be one of the most effective negative emotions. The DRAGONS attempt to use regret to entrench you in the past. Dr. Roese's research, however, confirms the positive nature of regret in that it provides a lens to make sense of the world and avoid known hazards by empowering you with the KINGDOM commodity called insight.

Insight allows you to maintain a KINGDOM-centered perspective on your life. Your past regrets do not define you. Insight allows you to visualize or imagine where your GODprint directs you, even when you do not yet see the physical manifestation. Visualization holds tremendous power in your pursuit of influence because it allows you to "see" and believe— even before the physical manifestation. Insight demagnetizes regret's backwards pull and releases you to envision who you were created to be before the foundation of the world.

<u>A</u>PATHY: THE DRAGONS' GRAVEYARD

By now, you understand the DRAGONS' intention to keep you away from your destiny. You have seen how self-doubt erodes your confidence in your true identity. You understand how regret keeps you heading in the wrong direction. The question, however, is where are the DRAGONS leading you? The answer is simple. They are leading you to the place where all dead things go — the graveyard.

When your physical body dies, your loved ones will memorialize and bury you in your earthly resting place. But the graveyard was never intended to be the final resting place of the wealth of our influence and passions. Les Brown, motivational speaker extraordinaire, captures the travesty of the graveyard in his oft-used illustration. "The graveyard is the richest place on earth, because it is here that you will find all the hopes and dreams that were never fulfilled, the books that were never written, the songs that were never sung, the inventions that were never shared, the cures that were never discovered, all because someone was too afraid to take that first step, keep with the problem, or determined to carry out their dream."[44]

Your GODprint is an investment that the Creator intended to outlive you. Your GODprint is not for the graveyard. Yet, that is exactly the DRAGONS' intent. This unfortunate fate is typically the product of apathy, or what you might think of as indifference. Apathy's deceit is genius. It destroys you by lulling you into a comfort zone of indecision encamped by a false sense of security. Apathy makes you think you are being prudent by leaving your options open or staying open-minded. In most situations, we like having options. We value open-mindedness. We, especially in Western cultures, consider this prudence. And, of course, in some situations it is exactly that.

However, the outgrowth of prolonged indecision is indifference. We fail to realize that sustained indecision is, in fact, a decision. You are deciding to live the status quo. That, of course, is a problem when you are called to be a person of

---

[44] Brown, L.; [cited 2015] Available from:
https://www.goodreads.com/quotes/884712-the-graveyard-is-the-richest-place-on-earth-because-it.

influence. At its most basic, it is a passive-aggressive maneuver that leaves you chasing your tail — running in circles, going nowhere. As I previously said, I am a runner. During the winter months, I primarily run indoors on the treadmill, usually for five miles. I feel the workout in every fiber of my body. Though my body has been subjected to an up-tempo experience, after all is said and done I am in the same place that I started. I do a lot of moving, but never leave the treadmill.

The Book of Joshua (5:6) records the sad story of the Hebrew people's treadmill life. After escaping the slavery of Egypt and while moving towards the land of Canaan (their "Promised Land"), the nation struggled with obedience to God. They allowed the DRAGONS to distort their sense of right and wrong. They lost their identity. Ultimately, rather than being able to cross the Jordan River and enter the land of promise, the historical records show they wandered in the wilderness for forty years until an entire generation went to the graveyard. The DRAGONS smiled. Only then did the Hebrew people exert the collective will to follow God's plan.

The longer I live, the more I see that this is exactly what many of us do. We live our lives, unwilling to commit to what it takes to unleash our GODprint. As time passes, we become indifferent. Regardless of the perceived risk, the reality is that you can only be fully alive when you are on the right side of your Jordan River. Your GODprint calls you to set trends, not treadmills.

ATTENTION TO NOVELTY

Apathy thrives in the familiar — the comfort zone. Aldous Huxley — English writer, philosopher, and one of the pre-eminent intellectuals of his time — made the profound statement, "familiarity breeds indifference."[45] When blinded by the excuses and blame characteristic of the comfort zone, we (like the Hebrew nation) wander in our own wilderness. The DRAGONS use apathy to put our minds on autopilot as they pertain to our GODprint.

Our brains are designed to allow us to operate efficiently in a complex world full of both major and minor decisions. We cannot give equal attention to everything. Our brain is a master dispatcher—alerting us to what needs our attention and what is rote. Every day, we make thousands of minor decisions about which we do not even consciously think. It is why you do not remember whether you locked the door, because you did it automatically. As a seasoned driver, you do not think about the mechanics of steering your car to your job. Your mind thought about many other things while you drove. Because these actions are familiar, you simply do not consciously think about them.

If the DRAGONS can consume you with life in the comfort zone among all that is familiar, in time your brain gets the message, "nothing new here." Your mind thinks tomorrow will be the same day as today and today is the same as yesterday. Day in and day out, everything feels the same. Indecision and indifference. The key is to make a decision to leave the rut, to do something novel, or new. When you make the decision to follow your GODprint, it can be painful. It can feel scary. However, it is the commitment to the decision that propels you through the obstacles.

One day, probably too soon, you will no longer be here—at some point, you and I will move on from this life. On that grave marker, there will be a place where your loved ones note your year of birth. For me, that was 1965. Then there will be the date that you died. But, between the year of your birth and death

---

[45]Huxley, A., *The Doors of Perception and Heaven and Hell.* 2004: Harper Perennial Modern Classics.

there is a dash (–). That dash represents everything meaningful that happened in your life. As people see your dash, what will they remember?

I guarantee you that it will not be degrees and positions that they remember. It is not how much money you had in your bank account. What they will remember about your dash is your GODprint. That will be your legacy. So, resurrect the decision to follow your passions and push apathy into that empty grave. Others are counting on you to live.

GUILT: THE DRAGONS' COLLECTOR

The American justice system is built on a fundamental premise that a person is innocent until proven guilty. Regardless of how egregious a felony, the prosecution must prove beyond a shadow of a doubt that the accused party indeed committed the crime. At least in Western cultures, this presumption of innocence dominates. Somebody, however, forgot to tell the DRAGONS.

Guilt is a type of cognitive dissonance and feeling state that emerges when our actions or thoughts are misaligned with a moral code to which we feel beholden. Simply put, when you fail to think or act in the way you believe, you should feel guilty.

The word guilt, which is of English origin, initially meant "debt" . . . and the DRAGONS are out to collect. But, first, let me tell you what the DRAGONS dare not speak. They will not tell you that there are two paths for guilt—one light and one dark. You have a choice. The DRAGONS will not inform you that you have the power to turn off the guilty spigot flooding your mind. No—the DRAGONS use guilt to keep you feeling as if you are in a perpetual state of psychological, spiritual, relational, and personal indebtedness. Furthermore, the DRAGONS make you feel devalued so that you never feel like you actually could measure up to the size of your debt.

95

The DRAGONS accomplish this by extolling the dark side of guilt, called condemnation. While it would be appropriate, within reason, to condemn misbehavior or an errant thought, this is not the DRAGONS' focus. The DRAGONS condemn who you are as a person. With each reminder of your past mistakes, poor decisions, and struggles, you feel that guilt's debt toll accrue higher.

The DRAGONS' guilt onslaught is relentless until you reach the point where you become so consumed with a sense of shame that it becomes the way you self-identify. Dr. Aaron Kipnis, psychologist and author of *Angry Young Men: How Parents, Teachers and Counselors Can Help Bad Boys Become Good Men*, says that shame's effects are more damaging than guilt. Kipnis continues, "Shame tends to direct individuals into destructive behaviors. When we focus on what we did wrong, we can correct it; but when we're convinced that we are wrong as a result of shame, our whole sense of self is eroded."[46] Shame erodes your sense of self—leaving your self-esteem and confidence in shambles. The DRAGONS use guilt to make you feel like a hypocrite and unworthy of your dreams. They may indeed use facts, but they will never tell you the truth.

CONVICTION AND THE POWER OF GRACE

We can find affirmation in the writings of the Apostle Paul in Romans 8:1, "There is therefore now no condemnation for those who are in Christ Jesus, who do not walk according to the flesh, but according to the Spirit" (NKJV). This faith perspective pulls us out of the self-centered morass and challenges us to consider who Christ says that we are. Your self-identity is not chained to the mistakes of your past. When you tap into your GODprint, it is conviction—not condemnation—that arises from guilt. This

---

[46] Kipnis, A., P. D., *Angry Young Men: How Parents, Teachers and Counselors Can Help Bad Boys Become Good Men.* 2002: Jossey-Bass.

conviction steers you towards acceptance, healing, and influence. Conviction is guilt's hopeful path and it serves a very functional role—engendering remorse about one's behavior. Guilt hopefully serves as a positive force here in holding you accountable and calibrating your behavior to avoid repeating the infraction. When functioning appropriately, this sense of conviction often pushes you towards repentance and possibly even restitution.

How can you resist the guilt trip that detours you away from your dream? That is the role of grace. Grace is undeserved favor. Grace acknowledges that you may feel a sense of indebtedness based on mistakes of your past. But, grace says that, despite those inadequacies, the debt is paid. Grace is selfless in that it recognizes that there is something bigger at work. Grace is the anathema to guilt and shame.

You do not have to make all of the right moves in your effort to follow your GODprint. You do not have to feel ashamed about past missteps. Grace is available in abundance along the road that your GODprint calls you. When you listen closely, you will hear God whisper words of grace to you. Graceful people will cross your path to encourage you. Just allow yourself to accept it and your GODprint will direct you to demonstrate it to others.

<u>O</u>BSTINANCE: THE DRAGONS' PRISON

No man is an island. Humans were designed to be in vital relationships with one another. However, the DRAGONS believe in isolation. Obstinance is a means through which this separation occurs. Obstinance is stubbornness and inflexibility that manifests as an unwillingness to compromise or consider the opinions of others. The DRAGONS depend on obstinance to fixate your mind on the status quo.

Earlier, we described how the fixed mindset sees choices as limited and opportunities as fleeting. In many ways, obstinance (and the fixed mindset from which it emanates) is as result of pride. John Maxwell says, "There are two kinds of pride, both good and bad. 'Good pride' represents our dignity and self-respect. 'Bad pride' is the deadly sin of superiority that reeks of conceit and arrogance."[47] I think Maxwell has nailed it. 'Bad pride' represents a separation from God—which is by nature the definition of sin. As one separates from God, he psychologically isolates from human relationships as well.

As you might imagine, the DRAGONS relish the fixed mindset because, at its core, it reeks of self-centeredness. How many people have a yearning inside for more in their life, only to self-sabotage by refusing to see what they are truly capable of achieving? At its best, this obstinance leads to a life of "should have been." At its worst, the fixed mindset devolves into a fatalistic posture characterized by chronic depression and, sometimes, suicide. Obstinance is an imprisoned mind that is shut off from the myriad of voices seeking to lift you. Outside opinions are devalued in favor of your own. You struggle even to hear from God. The longer you allow yourself to isolate your mind, the more difficult it will be for you to change course. But, it is never too late. You just have to learn the practice of deference.

DEFERENCE: THE LEARNING ACCELERATOR

Succinctly put, learning requires deference. Merriam-Webster's dictionary defines deference as "a way of behaving that shows respect for someone or something."[48] You can see

---

[47] Maxwell, J., "Pride - A leader's Greatest Problem," in Leadership Wired. 2007.
[48] Merriam-Webster. "Deference." [cited 2015] Available from: http://www.merriam-webster.com.

here why deference is the counter-response to obstinance. Obstinance stubbornly insists on its own way. Deference insists on honoring the input of another. While obstinance stunts your learning curve, deference accelerates it.

Accelerating your pursuit of influence is directly correlated with the degree to which you defer to others in your learning process. Whether through reading, listening, or watching trusted others, the individual who can best suspend his self-limiting beliefs and defer to experts' advice will best combat the DRAGONS' naysayers. In the process, you will not only learn more, but you will also develop trusted relationships with your benefactors. Additionally, those who master deference as a life and leadership skill also tend to be the ones who take responsibility for giving back in many other ways. Rather than stubbornly insisting on having things their way, these growth-minded individuals seek collective input because they understand that the whole is exponentially greater than the sum of its parts.

NARCISSISM: THE DRAGONS' REFLECTION

When people look at you, what do they see? The opening line to Rick Warren's New York Times bestseller, *The Purpose Driven Life*, reads, "It's not about you."[49] That is my favorite opening line of any book I have ever read. Your purpose neither begins nor ends with you. Your purpose is not about your ego, happiness, or social standing. Your purpose is about honoring your Creator and your neighbor by the authentic mobilization of your GODprint. The DRAGONS' purpose is to stop you from doing that.

If the DRAGONS were able to pen a counter-response to Pastor Warren, the book would probably be titled something like

---

[49] Warren, R., *The Purpose Driven Life: What on Earth Am I Here For?* 2002: Zondervan. pg. 1.

The Self-Centered Life with an opening line that reads, "It's all about you." As you have likely gleaned, the DRAGONS want you to believe that you are the center of your universe. The DRAGONS use narcissism to inflate your ego so that you view yourself as the ultimate arbiter of what is best for you. Of course, narcissism thrives on the comparison game—never content to feel second best.

The Diagnostic and Statistical Manual of Mental Disorders (DSM)-IV, which is used by clinicians to diagnose mental health disorders, defines narcissism as "a pattern of grandiosity, need for admiration, and a lack of empathy."[50] But, I like the Mayo Clinic's definition of the term: "a mental disorder in which people have an inflated sense of their own importance."[51] I cite these clinical definitions of narcissism to give you a sense of the most extreme manifestations of the condition. Most people are not so grandiose or callous. They would not fit the clinical criteria. But, the signs of self-centeredness, disregard for the plight of others, and sense of entitlement clearly show the DRAGONS' influence.

The irony, however, is that despite this veneer of bravado, narcissism leaves its victim with a fragile sense of self that often is unable to handle the slightest criticism. In order to avoid the pain of criticism, narcissism pushes you to take control, manipulate situations to avoid scrutiny, and deflect blame to others for any shortcomings. As with obstinance, narcissism isolates—pushing you into a cocoon that you consciously (or maybe subconsciously) believe protects you. In reality, it is

---

[50] American Psychiatric Association, Diagnostic and Statistical Manual of Mental Disorders-IV. 1994: American Psychiatric Publishing.
[51] Mayo Clinic. "Narcissistic personality disorder." [cited 2015] Available from: http://www.mayoclinic.org/diseases-conditions/narcissistic-personality-disorder/basics/definition/con-20025568.

sabotaging your GODprint and alienating you from the people that need you most.

REFLECTING THE OTHER

This section opened with a question of what people see when they look at you. I can tell you that what the DRAGONS want them to see is an empty shell that looks magnificent on the outside, but is rotting inside. What God wants them to see when they gaze at you is a reflection of themselves. If that sounds strange, bear with me as I explain.

Your GODprint always leads you in the direction of other people. Through these pages, you have seen how your GODprint encourages you to listen and empathize with the struggles of others. You have sensed the push of your GODprint to be authentic and open to sharing the highs and lows of your journey. Your real story holds the power to connect others to you — because they identify with you. In many of my own workshops, I have marveled as people have come up to me and told me how much my struggles sound just like theirs. Recently, when I was sharing some of the challenges in my marriage with a group of couples, I was startled as one of the male attendees burst out laughing. Initially, I was thinking to myself, why is he laughing at this quite somber failing of mine? He interjected that his laughter was just that of disbelief that he was struggling with exactly the same thing. He said, "It's like you have been in my house."

That is the promise of one's GODprint. We want others to feel like we have been in their house or in their shoes. That is the portrait of empathy. When people see you, they should see themselves. But, that is not where the story ends. Your story must ultimately return to your GODprint. As others see themselves in you, they are inspired by understanding your WHY. As they understand your WHY, they can more clearly see their own GODprint and pursue what the Creator has placed within them. These are the benefits of shunning those narcissistic tendencies and allowing your GODprint to move you towards those who can benefit from your voice. But remember: when people see you, you want them to see themselves first. Then, you want them to see the God in you.

SCARCITY: THE DRAGONS' MAGNIFIER

So, here we are, at the last of the DRAGONS. Last, but certainly not least. Actually, I consider scarcity the DRAGONS' magnifier because it is, in my opinion, the deadliest of the DRAGONS. All of the DRAGONS are pernicious. But, scarcity is like a highly infectious disease that makes all of the other DRAGONS "go viral." When magnified by scarcity, each of the DRAGONS becomes more self-centered, irrational, and greedy. Scarcity consumes you with an attitude of lack. No matter what, scarcity never has enough.

Scarcity takes one of two tactics, depending on your context. In a time of abundance, scarcity tells you to hoard and control all that you can because you never want to be in a position of lack. Scarcity tells you to "get it while the getting is good," as goes the idiom. Look out for number one. Scarcity says that if you don't take care of yourself, no one else will. Forget the needs of others. Scarcity believes in survival of the fittest. For scarcity, the idea of sharing your abundance with those in need is ludicrous. For scarcity, the motto is "every man for himself." Scarcity celebrates others' failures because it makes more available for him.

Jesus tells a parable, recorded in the Book of Luke. A rich man experienced an abundant harvest. Upon deliberation, he decided that since he did not have barns large enough to store his bounty, he would tear down his current barns and erect larger ones in their place. We can then see scarcity's influence in his remark, "And I will say to my soul, 'Soul, you have ample goods laid up for many years; relax, eat, drink, be merry.'" (Luke 12:19). Unfortunately for him, God calls him a fool and shows him the cost of his selfishness in stating, "This very night your life will be demanded from you." God condemns this rich fool for allowing a scarcity mindset to create a sense of self-sufficiency, greed, and apathy.

Scarcity not only flourishes in times of abundance but also in times of lack. In times of lack, scarcity keeps you focused on what you do not have. Scarcity tells the busy mom that she does not have time to pursue her passions. Scarcity tells the young singer that he isn't good enough to record his album. Scarcity tells the teenage girl that nobody will ask her to the prom because she's not pretty enough. Scarcity tells the grandfather that he doesn't have enough energy to spend the day with his grandchildren. Scarcity tells the second-year college student that he doesn't have enough money to finish his degree, so he might as well stop now.

Though, on the surface, it may look as if scarcity is different during times of abundance and times of lack, the truth is that it taps the same underlying problem—a lack of contentment. Scarcity's strategy is to make you associate your self-worth with self-sufficiency. Scarcity says that you are better or more secure if you have more stuff.

Scarcity magnifies the Doubt, Regret, Apathy, Guilt, Obstinance, and Narcissism to twist your mind into knots until you struggle to know whether you are coming or going. When your mental energy is consumed with what you do not have, you simply cannot focus on what you do have and where you are going. Thankfully, scarcity does not have the last say.

CONTENTMENT AND THE RESPONSIBILITY OF MUCH

It was previously noted that the root of scarcity is discontent. It should be no surprise then that scarcity's Achilles heel is contentment—that place where you are psychologically satisfied with who you are. That does not mean that you are not striving for bigger goals. Rather, it suggests that in the midst of that striving you feel good enough about who you are as a person, a family member, and a friend. You feel good enough about the direction that your life is moving. Not that you are perfect in any way. But, you are authentically heeding and enjoying the push of your GODprint without succumbing to the trappings of the culture's push for faster, bigger, and better things. Influential 19th-century preacher, theologian, and author Charles Spurgeon aptly says, "it is not how much we have, but how much we enjoy, that makes happiness."[52]

What is the opposite of scarcity? Most of us immediately think of abundance. But, I really appreciate the illumination of Dr. Brene Brown, author of *The Gifts of Imperfection: Let Go of Who You Think You're Supposed to Be and Embrace Who You Are*, as she stated, "For me, the opposite of scarcity is not abundance. It's enough. I'm enough."[53] Her point is well taken. The DRAGONS use scarcity to attack your personal sense of worth. But, when you confidently assert your sense of contentment with who you are in the presence of abundance or lack, you are saying, "I'm enough." This confidence helps you see life's riches that truly matter—authentically sharing a love of God, self, family, and community. With that blessing, you have much to offer. When you are faithful in your influence over these things, I am convinced that you will be given larger areas of influence.

Having much comes with a responsibility. The Bible tells us, "Everyone to whom much was given, of him much will be required" (Luke 12:48). As you are able to discern and show gratitude for how much you have, your GODprint will lead you

---

[52] Wikiquote. Charles Spurgeon. [cited 2015] Available from: https://simple.wikiquote.org/wiki/Charles_Spurgeon.
[53] Brown, B., *The Gifts of Imperfection: Let Go of Who You Think You're Supposed to Be and Embrace Who You Are*. 2010: Hazelden.

in how to share that with others. The more you are able to give to those in need, the more you will have. It may be money that you give. But, often the best gifts are when you are able to give your empathy, time, and talents.

You have been blessed with so much for which to be grateful. When scarcity and the rest of the DRAGONS spew their vile lies, your sense of contentment repels them. Anytime they reappear, remind yourself how much you have for which to be grateful. Neither you nor I are perfect. We are works in progress. But, even in the midst of this positive transformation we have enough character, integrity, love, and joy to influence others in the direction of their GODprint. Be encouraged. Go in the strength that you have. It is enough.

CHAPTER 7

SLAYING DRAGONS WITH A KINGDOM MINDSET

"Too many of us are not living our dreams because we are living our fears."

– LES BROWN

You have now extensively explored the DRAGONS' lair. You understand their manipulations. You know what to expect. If you wonder why we spent so much time focused on the DRAGONS, it is simply because they are the only things standing between you and your dreams. The only things. If you have an iota of skepticism as to their intention, ask yourself why you have yet to elevate to your next level. I challenge you to come up with even one excuse that is not related to the DRAGONS' deception.

The reality is that we all must journey through the DRAGONS' shadowlands. The journey of life has well-worn paths through their dark territory. It is unavoidable as it is intrinsically linked to the experience of being human. To live is to battle the DRAGONS, which is not necessarily a bad thing, for it is vital for your growth. You cannot be the hero of your life's story without defeating the DRAGONS.

You might be thinking to yourself that these DRAGONS are not real. They are all in one's mind. You are half right. They are in your mind, just as joy and anger are in your mind. They are in your mind, just like affirmation and abuse are in your mind. All of your experiences, real and imagined, are products of your brain's processing of them. So, yes, the DRAGONS are in your mind.

However, you would be wrong if you question the reality of their existence. Just one look at the trail of tears they cause in so many lives is proof enough of the DRAGONS' existence. The fragmented self is a defense mechanism — typically arising as a response to mental or physical anguish in early life experiences. Therapist calendars are filled with cases of individuals battling mental health challenges because of guilt's shaming at the hands of authoritarian parenting. On any given Sunday, church altars are visited by parishioners praying for faith to believe that God loves them, when they felt so unloved during their formative life stages. Every day in the workplace, we see co-workers jockeying to out-maneuver one another for the next promotion, no matter what the cost, driven by a subconscious need to feel validated. These are but a few practical examples of the DRAGONS' manipulations that are striking the deepest parts of our psyche.

The DRAGONS engage in psychological warfare. Each one of them works to get you mired in self — self-doubt, self-sufficiency, and self-pity. The result is a psychological phenomenon called splitting. This concept, first developed by Ronald Fairbairn in his formulation of Object Relations Theory, is the inability of an individual to see himself or others as simultaneously capable of both positive and negative qualities.[54]

---

[54] Wikipedia. "Splitting (psychology)." [cited 2015] Available from: https://en.wikipedia.org/wiki/Splitting (psychology).

Consequently, the split person experiences his world as one of extremes—all is wonderful or all is catastrophic. You can see the DRAGONS' handiwork. They use regret and guilt as supposed proof to convince you that you are all bad. There is nothing good to come of you. You don't even want to hear people who try to pull you from the funk. But, then the DRAGONS throw obstinance and narcissism your way to cloak you in a veneer of goodness. You put on a show. But, underneath you feel like a hypocrite.

The person struggling with such splitting not only sees themselves from an extreme perspective; they also see others through this polarizing lens—which makes their relationships quite unstable. In fact, the split person's psyche is often so fragile that, if someone dares criticize him, that critic is deemed a bad person and treated as a threat. Conversely, they may put the other person on an idealized pedestal and then vilify them when the person fails to live up to the unrealistic image.

The DRAGONS' battle for your mind has potential for extensive collateral damage. It is this fragmented view of one's person and life that most threatens one's true identity. It is the psychological polarization that allows the split person to compartmentalize their lives. We have all seen the pastor who struggles to control his anger at home, but then portrays himself as a paragon of purity at church. Maybe you have seen the salesperson who exudes uncanny confidence with her clients; however, her ego seems frail among family and friends. Hopefully, these perplexing examples will make more sense to you now that you see the DRAGONS' handiwork and understand the nature of the fragmented self.

> The integrated person is able to see their experiences as strengthening their character, resolve, and relationships.

BECOMING THE DRAGONS' SLAYER

This book was written to encourage you through the DRAGONS' shadowlands by affirming that each of their lies is offset by a powerful affirmation. You just have to invoke them. These affirmations, which were each introduced in the preceding chapter as a healthy response to the DRAGONS, empower you to have an integrated—rather than a fragmented—identity. An integrated person is one who is consciously aware of (and able to contain) both the good and bad parts of the past and the present. They are not in denial. But, they refuse to be defined as all good or all bad from these experiences. Despite the difficulties, the integrated person is able to see their experiences as strengthening their character, resolve, and relationships. The integrated person is able to convert their positive and negative experiences into empathy with healing properties. At their best, the integrated person shuns hypocrisy and is able to relate to others with realistic expectations. They accept that the nature of being human is to accept that, although sometimes people will give you joy, at other times they will cause pain. The integrated person shows the resolve to exist between these two realities and feels secure in their identity in the midst of the uncertainty.

How can you be an integrated person? It is best done by maintaining a KINGDOM perspective. Collectively, the first letter of each of the briefly introduced affirmations that we used against the DRAGONS spells KINGDOM.

- K is for Knowledge
- I is for Insight
- N is for Novelty
- G is for Grace
- D is for Deference
- O is for Other-centered
- M is for Much

The KINGDOM manifests as your internal GODprint manifests externally. I would like to offer both faith and secular perspectives on what it means to have a KINGDOM mindset.

First, from a faith perspective, KINGDOM refers to the Kingdom of God. In the Christian tradition specifically, this phrase is used 68 times in ten different New Testament books. God created you for a purpose—one that is different for each of us. But, ultimately, we all share a common one: to advance the Kingdom of God. We do that by listening and following the directions that God gives us to authentically connect with Him and with other people.

From a secular perspective, KINGDOM means that place where you feel fully alive because you are connecting with a cause that transcends you. The KINGDOM is that yearning for justice, freedom, and sharing, for you and those with shared passions. It is the place where you feel a sense of belonging and connectedness to your community. Dr. Brene Brown, author of Daring Greatly uses the term "wholeheartedness" to capture this KINGDOM mindset. For her, wholeheartedness is a byproduct of vulnerability and represents the capacity to engage in our lives with authenticity, cultivate courage and compassion, and embrace the imperfections of who we really are. Living authentically and embracing our imperfections is to be integrated. Allowing ourselves to courageously demonstrate compassion is advancing the work of the KINGDOM.

Regardless of whether you think about the KINGDOM from a faith or secular point of view, one thing that we will all agree on is that the systems of our world are not predicated on this transcendent mindset. Our world systems are primarily built upon the DRAGONS' philosophy of self-centered idolatry.

- The KINGDOM mindset espouses "we." The DRAGONS focus on "me."

- The KINGDOM mindset encourages giving. The DRAGONS speak of taking.
- The KINGDOM mindset enlists servants. The DRAGONS draft dictators.

In his excellent book, *The Upside-Down Kingdom*, author Donald Kraybill portrays how the Kingdom of God is truly antithetical to the social constructions of our day.[55] By leaning into these countercultural truths, we draw our strength from God rather than ourselves. We learn humility. We renew our mind. We understand that the weapons of our warfare are not of this world. They are of divine origin for the express purpose of slaying DRAGONS. Well, actually, the Bible says it this way: "We use God's mighty weapons, not worldly weapons, to knock down the strongholds of human reasoning and to destroy false arguments" (2 Corinthians 10:4, NLT). I like the way it is phrased in this translation because it clearly calls out the KINGDOM as a divine armory well equipped to obliterate the DRAGONS' "false arguments."

In the Bible's New Testament, the word repent is often used to describe that turning point from the ways of darkness to follow God's light. The Greek word for repent is *metanoia*, which literally means to change one's mind. A KINGDOM mentality is a continuous process of repenting of our lapses that give the DRAGONS a foothold and yearning for meaning that makes us come alive.

As we arm ourselves with this divine weaponry, we have the ammunition we need to advance God's purposes on Earth. The DRAGONS want you to think that it is about your strength. The KINGDOM perspective is about God's strength. The DRAGONS want you to believe that you do not have the pedigree for victory.

---

[55] Kraybill, D., *The Upside-Down Kingdom*. 1971: Herald Press.

> The KINGDOM perspective recognizes the ultimate truth: it is God's battle to fight, not yours.

The KINGDOM perspective acknowledges that it is not your strength that matters. The DRAGONS want you to see the battle as too big for you. But, the KINGDOM perspective recognizes the ultimate truth: it is God's battle to fight, not yours. I am inspired by God's words recorded in the Book of 2 Chronicles, "Listen, all Judah and inhabitants of Jerusalem and King Jehoshaphat: Thus says the Lord to you, 'Do not be afraid and do not be dismayed at this great horde, for the battle is not yours but God's'" (2 Chronicles 20:15). Listen, my friend, God has never lost a battle. As you follow your GODprint, I can assure you that God will not lose your battle either, if you let it be His to fight. Be encouraged, for He has anointed you as the DRAGONS' slayer.

CHAPTER 8

THE CREATION NATION

"Creativity is just connecting things. When you ask creative people how they did something, they feel a little guilty because they didn't really do it, they just saw something. It seemed obvious to them after a while."

– STEVE JOBS

You were born to create. Every creation takes on some aspect of its Creator. From the Book of Genesis we learn that God, the Creator, made you and me in His own image. Being created in the image of God means that there are certain aspects of God's nature that are wired into your DNA. One such attribute is creativity. We were designed to be creative. The difference, of course, between God and us is what in Latin is called creatio ex nihilo (creation out of nothing). In other words, God can create from nothing. In the Book of Genesis, we see that God simply spoke our world and humanity into existence. Whether it was light, water, or animals, God's decree to "let there be" was all that was necessary.

For us, however, we need something with which we can work. We cannot create out of thin air. Even our most masterful ingenuity is predicated on a set of physical or metaphysical material that already exists. We cannot create out of nothing. The beauty, however, is that through our relationship with Christ, we don't need this ability. What we have is the power to intercede to request God's hand in creating something from nothing. God still acts on our behalf.

It reminds me of a difficult time in the life of my family, when the OB/GYN told us that our efforts to have our second child were not going to happen. He diagnosed my wife, Dalia, with premature menopause. Her levels of follicle-stimulating hormones told a bleak story. Scientifically, we were unable to have children. We were devastated. But, we prayed. We asked friends and pastors to pray. We believed that God would intercede on our behalf. God answered those prayers and overrode what science declared. In our eyes, God created our precious daughter out of nothing. She is our miracle. At the follow-up visit after our daughter was born, the doctor admitted that he did not understand how that happened. He then proceeded to tell us that, according to science, we still should not be able to have children. The key to grasp here is that God is not bound by our rules and assumptions. He can and will create from nothing as He so wills.

> You have the power to creatively innovate because your GODprint taps into a divine source.

But, there is another point. God desires that we see our creativity as a reflection of His. You have the power to creatively innovate because your GODprint taps into a divine source. The question then isn't whether or not to create. But, there are other relevant questions to consider, such as, "What are you supposed to create?" This, of course, is driven by your passion. Another question is, "For whom are you to create?" Your creations are for your tribe—those who follow your voice. The next question is, "When are you supposed to create?" There is no hard and fast rule for that. But, I believe that you start creating as soon as you have an idea. That creation can then evolve as your idea matures. Too many people wait too long to start creating — erring in waiting for a fully formed idea before they take the first step. That is a colossal mistake that allows the DRAGONS to keep you on the sidelines rather than in the game. Take the step to create. Clarity comes during the creation process.

I experienced this even while writing this book. I struggled for many months to really get started, because I was trying to conceptualize the entire book before I started. I wasted a lot of time because I could not see the whole thing. However, once I just started writing every day without fail, guess what happened? The sections and chapters started to emerge. I have learned through this process to trust that the finished product will be revealed to me just in time. That is the faith element of creativity.

In fact, there is a major lesson here. When we try to figure everything out in our own timing, relying on our own strength, we are often frustrated. Over time, that frustration can turn into disillusionment and, ultimately, detachment from your core purpose. The problem, however, is a failure to release your assumptions and your will. However, when we trust God's direction and timing, we put that weight on Him, thus freeing ourselves of that pressure. It says that we believe that which we do not see. It communicates trust in what God has spoken to us, more than in our own abilities. With this perspective, we are able to maintain a sense of creative contentment.

The Apostle Paul encourages us to learn to be content in whatever state we find ourselves in, writing, "Not that I was ever in need, for I have learned how to be content with whatever I have. I know how to live on almost nothing or with everything. I have learned the secret of living in every situation, whether it is with a full stomach or empty, with plenty or little" (Philippians 4:11–12, NLT). That attitude of contentment is critical because it provides you the psychological space to create. Psychological space means an unencumbered mindset. Think of writer's block as an example. When the words are not freely flowing, the writer feels stuck. But, at some point the "writer's block" itself becomes the problem. The writer becomes so focused on the "writer's block" that no writing happens. What was a small challenge becomes a psychological mountain. But, when the writer is able to ease the pressure that he has placed on himself to beat the monstrous "writer's block" and just allows his mind to settle, the words will flow again. Whether internally- or externally-derived, pressure stunts creativity.

Imagine the challenge of people who are tasked to produce creative works in adrenaline-filled corporate offices with unforgiving schedules. I've worked with many of these creatives in pressure-ridden contexts. There is no doubt that their best work is sacrificed on the altar of expediency. In my own day job, I experience this same challenge. The higher the pressure, the more difficult it is to think creatively. Few things are more foreboding at work than the blank page staring at me as an important deadline looms. The only way to recover is to take control of your thoughts and create mental space for contentment. Release the pressure by placing your circumstance and its emotional tension into God's hands. You can trust him to be there for you. You can be content in God's provision. As promised in Deuteronomy 31:6, "Be strong and courageous. Do not fear or be in dread of them, for it is the Lord your God who goes with you. He will not leave you or forsake you." God will not leave you nor forsake you. Relax. Release. Contentment releases creativity.

CREATION OUT OF NOTHING

We often limit God's ability to unleash the creativity within us because we refuse to release our efforts to Him. We want to wield as much control as possible over our inputs and the outputs. We want to feel confident in the rational merit of our situation. We want to feel that our creative efforts are within our reach, even if it requires us to stretch a little bit. But, those are not ideal operating conditions for God. God prefers to create something from nothing. He relishes in those opportunities to shine in the impossible situations of our lives. He moves in those spaces that make no sense and defy rational and scientific explanation—as in the case of my daughter's miraculous birth.

Why does God like to create from nothing? It's actually quite simple. God desires that our creativity speaks to humanity about His goodness. Our creativity is intended to point people to God and help them connect with Him. This simply means that your creativity is not for you. It is for God. He gave it to you for His own glory and for the edification of your community. If you could control the creativity of your own volition, you probably would not attribute that success to God.

> The only way to be obedient to God is to co-create with Him.

Most of us fail in that regard . . . we want to take the credit. We want to believe that our creative successes are a product of our own initiative, brilliance, connections, and resources. But, extraordinary influence is ultimately a testimony to God's work in your life. You see, creativity is not optional. It is essential to Christian living. The only way to be obedient to God is to co-create with Him.

To fully grasp this notion, however, you must grasp creativity's meaning. Creativity is often misunderstood. We tend to think of creative people as artists (e.g., painters) or performers (e.g., singers). Those types of people certainly are creative. But, creativity is more ubiquitous than that. Creativity is everywhere from the Samsung Galaxy smartphone in our pockets to the ships that explore the galaxies of outer space. Creativity connects community, whether social media communities on Facebook and Twitter, or local neighborhood rallies to improve social conditions.

> Your imaginative capacity is your greatest asset because it is the blueprint for innovation.

Creativity is the expression of your imagination and expertise. When considered more generally, creativity is the use of the imagination to transcend traditional thinking. This creativity can then be applied in many different areas. In the next chapter, you will have the opportunity to consider the many ways in which the creativity of your GODprint can be expressed. When you are able to liberate it from the DRAGONS, your imaginative capacity is your greatest asset because it is the blueprint for innovation. Creativity is what allows you to see new ways of doing familiar things. But, creativity is also inspiring people to believe in something that was previously seen as unattainable. Creativity is the lens through which you experience and engage the world around you. In that way, creativity is divine because it views challenges with people and circumstances from a solution-centered, rather than problem-centered, point of view. As evidenced by our GODprint, God sees all of us from a creative perspective—which is why in the Book of Psalms we are described as "fearfully and wonderfully made"(139:14).

Any successful pursuit of influence is predicated on creativity, because to truly lead is to create or chart a new path. That is creativity at its most basic. There is plenty of empirical literature dissecting the difference between leadership and management. But, think of it this way. If you simply protect the status quo, that is not leadership. That is management, and creativity is not necessarily required. Transforming your life and the lives of others demands fresh and novel approaches to life's challenging questions. It requires a different way of thinking. Transformational leaders esteem creativity as indispensable.

Serial entrepreneur Derek Fagerstrom and his wife Lauren Smith are an excellent example of creativity applied in the business context. In an interview with Fast Company, Fagerstrom contrasts how, in years past, creative people limited their imagination to artistic endeavors in areas such as music, drawing, painting, and film. But, Fagerstrom notes that "people no longer think of business as the antithesis of art, but as an opportunity to express their vision."[56] Over the past twenty years, this couple has founded several small businesses as they have followed their own passions. They curated the work of their artist friends at The Curiosity Shoppe in San Francisco, launched a live event series called Pop-Up Magazine, and rehabilitated a quaint movie theater in Russian River, California. As reported in Fast Company, "Fagerstrom considers these projects his creative contribution to the world."[57]

CREATION NATION

Creation nation is the global community of those who embrace their creative identity to make the world a better place.

Fagerstrom is right. Each of us is challenged to consider our creative contribution to the world. Each person is called to be

---

[56] Segran, E. *From Passion to Profit: How to Make Money Doing What You Love.* 2015; Available from:
http://www.fastcompany.com/3045857/passion-to-profit/from-passion-to-profit-how-to-make-money-doing-what-you-love.
[57] Ibid.

creative. Creativity is not limited to Greenwich Village, Silicon Valley, and Hollywood. I like to think of us collectively as a creation nation. Creation nation is the global community of those who embrace their creative identity to make the world a better place. But, in order to know your own path in this creation nation, you must first know what type of creative you are. While the creative possibilities are limitless, I suggest that all creatives fall into one or more of four categories. While creatives share some characteristics, such as an active imagination, each has a particular orientation that distinguishes it. If you are like most, one of these categories will feel most like you. Personally, my GODprint leads me to pursue influence as a "Builder." I enjoy writing books, developing frameworks and conceptual models, and conducting workshops that help people connect disparate things in order to create that "aha" moment.

Consider these four types of creative people. Which of these categories best describes the direction of your GODprint? Some of you will see aspects of yourself in more than one. But, which one captures you at your best?

FOUR TYPES OF CREATIVES

1. Builders

Builders create products and services. They are called builders because they "build" physical or digital products (e.g., books, software, tools) or provide services (e.g., therapy, consulting) that educate, entertain, or otherwise assist others. Examples include legendary builders like Steve Jobs with Apple or Bill Gates with Microsoft, whose products (e.g., the iPod and Windows respectively) changed the world. But, builders are pervasive. As author of this book and others, I am a builder. But, think of the number of books that are written in one year in the United States alone. Estimates suggest that between 600,000 and one million books are written each year. Forbes magazine suggests that more than 500,000 new businesses are started each month in the United States. That's more than six million new businesses each year—though, admittedly, an astronomical number of those businesses have limited financial success. The point, however, is that there are millions of builders that are offering a product or service to their physical or virtual community. Builders' creativity is expressed through the innovation of these product and service offerings. If your desire is to influence through products and services that you create, then you are a builder. Your mission, then, is to allow your GODprint to direct you to build with a spirit of innovation—satisfying the needs of those who follow your voice.

2. Advocates

Advocates create a conversation or movement. They challenge social assumptions to promote justice, empower the disenfranchised, or otherwise champion a worthwhile cause. Abraham Lincoln (anti-slavery), Mother Teresa (eliminating poverty), and Mahatma Gandhi (Indian independence) are each examples of advocates with international acclaim.

On the morning of June 5th, 1989, a single man known today only as "tank man" stood up against the powerful Chinese military in Tiananmen Square. As the lead tank attempted to move on the square, he stood his ground. When the lead tank in the column sought to maneuver around him, "tank man" repeatedly moved in front of the tank to obstruct its path. This remarkable standoff was filmed and broadcast globally to depict the resistance against the Chinese government's violent crackdown against the protestors. "Tank man" was a creative. Without intending to do so, he created a symbol of resistance against human rights violations that will long be remembered around the globe.

I recently interviewed Kim Trumbo, founder of the Generosity Philosophy Podcast. Kim uses her platform to highlight heroes who live to give. In my conversation with Kim, we discussed her desire that this podcast be part of an international movement to bring attention to the many ways in which humans give of themselves. Through her podcast, her website, and her lively personality, Kim creates a conversation and a movement of generosity. We are all enriched by it.

"Tank man" and Kim are just two examples of millions of people who advocate for change or acknowledgment—often against established cultural norms and sometimes with certain personal costs. Thankfully, the Internet allows "tank man," Kim Trumbo, and the millions of other global advocates—for the rights of children, against human trafficking, and against genocidal governments—to galvanize support for their cause. Advocates create resistance against apathy, ignorance, and abuses. In doing so, they connect humanity to a transcendent and unifying truth.

3. Aesthetics

Aesthetics create an atmosphere. Atmosphere refers to the emotionality of a setting. Aesthetics personify, within their context, the beauty of the culture. In varied ways, they connect us to our emotional core. In Chapter 3, we talked about the Michaels (Michael Jordan, Michael Jackson, and Michael Flatley). Jordan's basketball prowess and tenacity was electrifying during many of his years in the NBA on his route to six championship titles. Michael Jackson's music continues to move our feet as well as our hearts, inspiring a new generation of fans, even years after his untimely death. Maya Angelou, with works such as "I know why the caged bird sings" and Luciano Pavarotti (dubbed "King of the High C" for his classic aria Pour mon âme) are other examples of aesthetics.

But, you do not have to be a celebrity to be an aesthetic. My mom, Dorothy P. Arnold, is an aesthetic. She can walk into a room of complete strangers, and, after two hours, everyone in the room knows Dorothy. When she caters to the gregarious part of her personality, the force of her personality and other aesthetics set the tone of the room. Aesthetics create an atmosphere that touches our souls.

4. Networkers

Networkers create social hubs. They apply their gifts to connect people. In his New York Times bestseller, *The Tipping Point,* author Malcolm Gladwell calls them "Connectors."[58] Gladwell describes them as the kinds of people who know everyone. This knowledge is used to refer people to the right person or service. They love talking with people for the sake of talking. Connectors are social hubs whose burgeoning relational network facilitates information and power transfer. Networkers get their greatest pleasure from putting people in meaningful relationships. These are the type of people who never seem to meet someone that they don't like. And, they seem to know everyone.

Pam Perry, public relations and social media expert, is a networker. One conversation with Pam inevitably leads you down a rabbit trail of people who you just must meet. Pam is a wealth of knowledge and source of inspiration, and she always knows someone to whom she can refer you. That obviously benefits her as a public relations strategist. But, one need not dig deep to see that Pam does not reserve this gift for her paying clients. Pam loves people. And, she clearly sees her God-given purpose in life as helping these people discover each other — especially when it helps them get their message out to the world.

---

[58] Gladwell, M., *The Tipping Point: How Little Things Can Make a Big Difference.* 2006: Little, Brown and Company. p. 38.

To say that Networkers create friendships is like saying that Michael Flatley created an Irish dance. Flatley revolutionized and popularized Irish dance through some fundamental innovations. Networkers revolutionize culture by connecting creatives to one another and inspiring a synergistic effect that would otherwise not exist. In this way, Networkers facilitate and expedite the efficiency at which creativity manifests.

THE GREATEST CREATION

Given that you and I are created in the image of God, we are imbued with a creative DNA. Our job is to co-create with the Maker. Naturally, this creation is intended to reflect your inner Bee (as discussed in Chapter 3). The details look different for each of us. But, without question, you are here to create an experience for someone. And, through this experience you mature in your relationship with God, with your community, and with yourself.

Regardless of which type of creative you are, there is one thing that we are each here to create. That one thing is "value." Whether you are a Builder, Advocate, Aesthetic, or Networker, you are ultimately creating value for your tribe. You add value to their lives by touching an emotional need. A Builder adds value by creating a product or service that makes it possible or easier to do a desired job. An Advocate adds value and connects us to our humanity by creating dissonance with injustices or the status quo. An Aesthetic adds value by creating beauty that elevates our spirits. Finally, a Networker adds value through collective synergy. It is all about adding value to the lives of others because, in doing so, you touch an emotional core that encourages them to engage you and your message.

As an influencer, your greatest objective (and, as such, your greatest creation) is adding value. When value is present, accessible, and appropriately packaged, everything else takes care of itself. Whether your influence is pursued on the first or second shift, value is the great differentiator. Many people are producing content. Many are seeking to build influential platforms. Long-term success, however, will only come to those who consistently add value. In the next chapter, you will see many possible ways that you can creatively add value to your tribe. Use it to strengthen your own value proposition. Whether the ultimate breadth of your influence is dozens or millions, when you add value you create a spark in another person. That spark can then ignite a revolution.

PART 3:

THE SOUND OF INFLUENCE

CHAPTER 9

LISTEN EMPHATICALLY

"Seek first to understand, then to be understood."

— STEPHEN COVEY

In his New York Times bestseller, *The 7 Habits of Highly Effective People*, author Stephen Covey encourages us to embrace understanding before striving to be understood.[59] We have five senses (seeing, hearing, touching, smelling, and tasting) — each of which contributes significantly to our quality of life and the way that we understand the world. If you had to choose one of your senses as most important for your survival, which one would you pick? Many people will say the ability to see. After all, vision is the most complex of our senses. When I was younger, I used to wonder to myself whether I would prefer to give up my sight or my hearing. Ultimately, I always concluded that I would rather have my sight because it would enable me to be more independent. But, there is compelling evidence that hearing and listening may be most important to our survival (and our influence).

Brown University neuroscientist, Dr. Seth Horowitz — who is among the nation's foremost authority on hearing — posits that it

---

[59] Covey, S., *The 7 Habits of Highly Effective People: Powerful Lessons in Personal Change*. 1990: Simon Schuster.

is our ability to hear that is our most important and evolved sense and "is a more essential tool for survival than sight."[60] That was a provocative conclusion to me—particularly coming from a scientist who studies brain imaging as his profession. Horowitz's argument is that hearing has been more fundamental to human survival because, in many ways, our ability to hear provides an auditory warning signal while the threat remains outside of our field of vision. In other words, you could hear something coming even before you could see it. Similarly, if you are hunting for food, you may hear the rustle of the bushes to alert you that prey is nearby, even though you are still unable to see it. He continues, "While it might take you a full second to notice something out of the corner of your eye, turn your head toward it, recognize it and respond to it, the same reaction to a new or sudden sound happens at least 10 times as fast." So, whether hunting or being hunted, the ability to hear is fundamental to survival. But, what about the ability to listen?

Listening—the ability to accurately receive and interpret messages in the communication process—is a lost art in our culture. Whether in the workplace, home, or community, everyone wants to be heard. But, too often, very few want to listen. We instinctively want to get our point across. For some of us, we just believe that if we can get the other person to hear the facts, then they will see it our way. Others believe that if we can just get them to understand why this is important to us, then they will get it. Unfortunately, what ensues is what can best be visualized as fire hoses gushing water at one other. Each person gushes with the conviction that the other should be listening. Except, they mostly aren't. The only thing truly happening in that exchange is that everyone is getting wet. I like the saying

---

[60] Horowitz, S., "The Science and Art of Listening." 2012 [cited 2015]; Available from:
http://www.nytimes.com/2012/11/11/opinion/sunday/why-listening-is-so-much-more-than-hearing.html?smid=pl-share&_r=0.

that God gave us two ears and one mouth, indicating that we should be listening twice as much as speaking. And, listening isn't just a physiological process of sounds vibrating across your ear drum. No, listening is a relational process of trying to put yourself in the shoes of the speaker (empathy).

But, we struggle to listen for several reasons. First, because we are often so self-centered that we prioritize speaking over listening. This happens when we over-value what we have to say; we generally feel like, if people only knew what we knew, then they would be so much better off. As you might surmise, this thinking is faulty, to say the least. Though it goes against our primal instinct, when it comes to encouraging others we are much more effective when we just allow them to express themselves without fear of reprisal of judgment. Secondly, we struggle to listen because we put too much faith in seeing, which inevitably comes at the expense of listening. I described this tendency when highlighting the DRAGONS' strategy for undermining our faith. But, to recap, when we are socialized to place our faith primarily in what we see, we compromise the benefits of our other senses. Listening offers more potential for insight than seeing, because it better accounts for environmental and personal nuances that are at play. With broader insight, a more well-rounded situational assessment is possible—an assessment that can more readily incorporate one's faith narrative. However, when seeing suppresses listening, one is only left with a one-dimensional perspective. The final reason I believe that we struggle to listen is, frankly, ignorance.

> The difference between hearing and
> listening is attention.

So many of us do not distinguish between hearing and listening. So, we are fooled into thinking that we are listening when, in fact, we are not . . . we are only hearing. Let's take a step back to clarify this distinction between listening and hearing. It is important for us to comprehend our ability to encourage and influence from the second shift.

THE ROLE OF ATTENTION

The difference between hearing and listening is attention. While this may sound rather simple, it is actually rather complex. Dr. Horowitz explains in the article, "The Art and Science of Listening," that there are three different ways in which you pay attention when your brain processes auditory sound. The most primal is the startle response. We have all been in that situation when a loud noise erupts unexpectedly and our body tenses. That noise certainly got our attention. But, as Dr. Horowitz explains, "A chain of five neurons from your ears to your spine takes that noise and converts it into a defensive response in a mere tenth of a second—elevating your heart rate, hunching your shoulders and making you cast around to see if whatever you heard is going to pounce and eat you. This simplest form of attention requires almost no brains at all and has been observed in every studied vertebrate." Dr. Horowitz goes on to explain that a more complex type of attention to auditory input occurs when someone calls your name or an unexpected birdcall is whistled in a subway station. "This stimulus-directed attention is controlled by pathways through the temporoparietal and inferior frontal cortex regions, mostly in the right hemisphere—areas that process the raw, sensory input, but don't concern themselves with what you should make of that sound." Neuroscientists label this brain engagement as "bottom up" response. Finally, there is the most complex type of attention that neuroscientists label "top down" response, in which you deliberately pay attention to an auditory input. This type of attention is really what we mean when we describe listening. These auditory signals are conveyed through a dorsal pathway in your cortex, part of the brain that does more computation, which lets you actively focus on what you're hearing and tune out sights and sounds that aren't as immediately important—at least until some bottom-up or startle response overrides it.

The message here is that, while our hearing has been critical to our survival since the beginning of mankind, our ability to listen attentively is essential for the survival and promulgation of our influence. When we focus on what someone is saying to us, we allow our brains to fully process the information—which fosters understanding. Stephen Covey's admonition to seek understanding first only happens when we give our focus to the matter or person to whom we are listening—allowing us to empathize. Generally, the old adage is true that people want to know how much you care before they care how much you know. And, caring is best communicated by attentive listening.

> The workplace advantages of better listening
> have been shown to be customer satisfaction,
> greater productivity, and increased creativity.

The workplace advantages of better listening have been shown to be customer satisfaction, greater productivity, and increased creativity according to Skillsyouneed.com. In fact, billionaire and Virgin airlines founder Richard Branson frequently attributes his tremendous success to his ability to listen. One certainly cannot question his success. Of course, the advantages of listening are also relevant in home and community settings as well. Marva Shand-McIntosh—a personal friend, speech pathologist, and founder of the national I Love to Listen Day (May 16th)—offers some great wisdom on listening on her website, Ilovetolisten.com. And, her ten listening tips are particularly helpful for parents in working with children.[61] The message here, of course, is that listening has tremendous value from the youngest child in the home to the seasoned veteran in the workplace. There is certainly biblical precedent for this in James 1:19, in which the author admonishes, "let every person be quick to hear, slow to speak, slow to anger." In other words, listening happens fastest. Maybe that is why God created us with an auditory capacity that reacts so quickly to environmental cues. Just as quickly as we should embrace listening, we should be just as slow to put in our "two cents' worth."

THREE LISTENING PRACTICES

Influence always begins with the practice of listening, regardless of the shift on which your passion is pursued. But, an effective listening practice is particularly critical on the second shift because of the constraints within which it must occur. It helps you more deftly navigate those time, resource, and relational margins that we earlier described. While listening is the necessary first node on your journey towards greater second-shift influence, it is important to understand that listening must first begin internally. More specifically, it requires that you listen to who the Creator made you to be (your GODprint). That must be the starting point. Otherwise, nothing else makes sense. But, as you attune to the direction of your GODprint, you can more clearly discern and master the three listening practices essential to your second-shift success.

I would like to offer an illustration to clarify this effect. Imagine that your GODprint is an antenna of sorts — figuratively akin to one you might see on a conventional citizens band (CB) radio. Though widely popular in the 1970s in the United States,

---

[61] Osula, M.S.-M.B. "Ten Listening Tips for Parents and Guardians." [cited 2015] Available from: http://www.ilovetolisten.com/ten-tips.

other technological advances have largely relegated CB usage to long-distance truckers. As expected of a mobile communications device such as the CB, the functionality of the device depends on the antenna, which is capable of both emitting and receiving radio communications. Your passion is to your GODprint what the antenna is to the CB radio. The longer the antenna, the stronger the signal it can detect. Similarly, the stronger or deeper your passion, the farther it can reach—limited only by your imagination and conviction. To continue with the analogy, the antenna of passion is designed to detect others who emit a similar signal or those in need of your passions. However, the strength of your antenna of passion determines its operating range. In other words, if your passion lacks a strong fervor, your antenna will have a very short range. You might pick up on obvious connections that are in your immediate vicinity, but you are likely to miss out on more subtle cues. Conversely, if your passion is fiery, your antenna's range extends far beyond your physical location. You can leverage technology and relationships to reach those who you cannot see or may not even know.

Your antenna of passion is the conceptual construct that allows you to develop the three listening practices that position you for maximum second-shift influence. The antenna of passion not only keeps you connected to your core identity and passion, but it also leads you to your tribe—a community of people with similar passions. I encounter so many people who are troubled that they do not know their passion or that they are not operating within their passion. I firmly believe that this dissatisfaction is a result of people operating out of the range of their own passions. They feel out of place because their antenna is not picking up any signal. If that describes you, be encouraged, because it is just a matter of fanning those internal flames and getting your antenna operating as it is designed to do. That is the focus of the next three chapters. These chapters examine the three listening practices that both affirm your

GODprint and position you to wield its influence to become the person you were created to be.

- Listening Practice #1: Follow the sound of passion—this practice clarifies your identity and encourages you to follow a path where you can remain authentic to who you are at your core.
- Listening Practice #2: Train your ear—this practice encourages you to be optimally attentive and attuned to your inner voice and the voices of those who you are called to influence.
- Listening Practice #3: Craft your voice—this practice encourages you to hone your voice to speak with authority that transforms lives.

Regardless of the setting in which you find yourself, dedicate yourself to becoming the best listener in the room. As you do, you will hear and truly understand the pulse of your people.

CHAPTER 10

FOLLOW THE SOUND OF PASSION

"Passion is one great force that unleashes creativity, because if you're passionate about something, then you're more willing to take risks."

– YO-YO MA

Many individuals struggle to be influential because they are lost — unsure of their own purpose in life. For them, today was like yesterday and yesterday like the day before. They expect tomorrow to be no different than today. The first key to increasing your influence is to truly listen to the cry of your soul. For what does it long? What gives you joy and makes you come alive? This is your passion. When you listen to the sound of your own passion, it naturally leads you to others who are attracted to that same sound. There is your community — or what Seth Godin coined your "tribe" in his bestseller, *Tribes: We Need You to Lead Us.*[62] Many people struggle because they are distracted by the sound of other people's passions — rather than their own. The reality is this: If you don't follow the sound of your own passion, you will be paralyzed and disoriented in a cacophony of noise coming from everyone else.

---

[62] Godin, S., *Tribes: We Need You to Lead Us.* 2008: Portfolio.

The 'sound of passion' has a nice, almost poetic, ring to it. But, what does it really mean? Does passion have a sound? I am convinced that it does. I was on the phone with Dixie Gillespie, author of *Just Blow It Up: Firepower for Living an Unlimited Life* and editor at the popular online portal, The Good Men Project. Though Dixie and I had exchanged emails with each other, that was our first live conversation. And, it was like we were old friends. We talked about our backgrounds, our drive for helping people tap into their own passion, our faith journeys, and much more. What brought Dixie and me together? It was the sound of passion. A mutual friend knew both of our passions and introduced us. But, how did that friend know that Dixie and I would hit it off so well? I contend that it is the sound of passion.

> Passion usually emerges from
> the suffering in your life.

The sound of passion is an emotionally magnetic energy pulsating within and around people in active pursuit of their dream or what they love doing. The sound of passion is like a buzz or hum that attracts people of similar interests and aspirations. Think about the bees of influence described in Chapter 3. Bees buzz. That buzz that we hear from bees is the rapid wingbeats that create wind vibrations, which people hear as buzzing. Passionate people also create a buzz. Like the bees' wingbeats, when your passion beats, it stirs the atmosphere and creates an energy that is palpable. You can feel it. Within five minutes of talking with my new friend Dixie, my ears were consumed by the buzz. My heart was racing with excitement. As we talked, a myriad of ideas was flooding my mind. I was alive.

We have talked extensively about passion in previous chapters. When we speak of passion, we think of it as a fiery internal feeling—and it is. But, there is a richer dimension of passion. Yes, passion is intense and compelling internal enthusiasm. But, passion is also relational. The original meaning of the word passion is "to suffer or endure" and has linguistically evolved to mean a "strong emotion or desire." It is helpful to look at both of these definitions in thinking about the origin of our own passion. Why is it so integral to who you are? Well, it is because your passion usually emerges from the suffering in your life. Usually that suffering is physical, emotional, relational, or a combination of those.

When I look at my own passion for helping marriages and families, I can clearly see the connection to the emotional and relational wounds of my youth. My parents' marriage has been a struggle for them for my entire life. Though I am thankful that they have endured the trials, their battles left scars on their children — especially me, being the eldest. My mother's exasperation with my father was often taken out on me. During my teen years, when it came to my mother, I felt angry, unfairly treated, and unloved. Even as a teenager, I vowed that I would not have a marriage like my parents'. As I got older and saw many people struggling with marriage, those deep-seated emotions within me were triggered. I wanted to be a positive force against dysfunctional marriages and families, rather than feel like the victim of my youth. This desire led me to pursue graduate training as a marriage and family therapist.

Though I never pursued licensure in the profession, I have established myself as an author and authority in this field. As such, I have had the opportunity to speak to thousands of married and engaged couples in diverse settings. In this capacity as a relationship educator, I have the opportunity to interact with many other people with a similar passion for meaningful family life, leadership development, and Christian stewardship. When in the company of people with similar passions, I come alive.

Despite the difficulty of working with couples — especially those in distress — I am drawn to the buzz because it speaks to my internal GODprint. I enjoy voraciously reading, learning, and teaching about leadership because the buzz is intoxicating. I find a deep satisfaction amidst the hum of like-minded others that seek a life of integrity and wholeheartedness; there is a buzz among those with a Christ-centered worldview that eschews many of society's cultural trappings. While this buzz may sound like an esoteric kumbaya, there is actually a strong physiological explanation for it. This buzz to which I refer is actually the product of four brain chemicals—dopamine, oxytocin, serotonin, and endorphins. I do not believe there is any greater indication that we are wired to follow the sound of passion than to understand that our biological neurotransmitters actually attune to the buzz.

THE BIOLOGY OF THE BUZZ

In his groundbreaking book, *The Rise of Superman: Decoding the Science of Ultimate Human Performance*, author Steven Kotler—extolled as one of the world's leading experts on human performance—convincingly describes how the human ability to accomplish extraordinary feats is a result of what is now called "flow." Through the work of the Flow Genome Project and the availability of neurological imaging technology, Kotler and his colleagues have been able to demonstrate flow as an optimal state of consciousness, a peak state where we both feel our best and perform our best. As Kotler continues, "In flow, we are so focused on the task at hand that everything else falls away. Action and awareness merge. Time flies. Self vanishes. Performance goes through the roof." Kotler and colleagues "call this experience 'flow' because that is the sensation conferred. In flow, every action, each decision, leads effortlessly, fluidly, seamlessly to the next."[63] While much of the study of flow has revolved around the death-defying acts of extreme and adventure athletes, the Flow Genome Project has worked to demonstrate the applicability of flow in heightening workplace performance and social relationships more broadly.

I am enamored with this notion of flow because I believe that it explains the feeling that we get when experiencing the buzz of passion on our internal antenna. Whether describing flow or the buzz of passion, they originate from the same source—biological chemicals surging through our brains. The buzz is biological—neurochemical, to be exact. As Kotler explains, "at a very simple level, neurochemicals are 'information molecules' used by the brain to transmit messages that are either excitatory or inhibitory." Excitatory impulses say do more of this, while inhibitory ones say do less of that. While there are a number of neurochemicals involved in flow, we will focus on the four that author Simon Sinek, in his New York Times bestseller, *Leaders Eat Last: Why Some Teams Pull Together and Others Don't*, describes as contributing to all our happy feelings: dopamine, oxytocin, serotonin, and endorphins.

As Sinek explains, "whether acting alone or in concert, in small doses or large, anytime we feel any sense of happiness or joy, odds are it is because one or more of these chemicals is coursing through our veins."[64] And, as evidence of the internal and external significance of our GODprint and passion, Sinek highlights how two of these hormones—dopamine and endorphines—"work to get us where we need to go as individuals." He calls these the "selfish" chemicals. The other two hormones—oxytocin and serotonin—"are there to incentivize us to work together and develop feelings of trust and loyalty." He

---

[63] Kotler, S., *The Rise of Superman: Decoding the Science of Ultimate Human Performance*. 2014: New Harvest. pg. viii.
[64] Sinek, S., *Leaders Eat Last: Why Some Teams Pull Together and Others Don't*. 2014: Portfolio. pg. 37.

dubs these the "selfless" chemicals. These selfless chemicals work together to facilitate social bonding.

One of the key components of the neurochemical cocktail responsible for flow includes dopamine, which is released whenever we take a risk or encounter something novel. Dopamine rewards and helps us survive exploratory behavior by increasing attention, information flow, and pattern recognition. Dopamine makes us goal-oriented and plays a role in reward-motivated behavior. Most types of reward increase the level of dopamine in the brain. As Sinek describes, "that feeling of progress or accomplishment is primarily because of dopamine." As an example of dopamine's power, the highly addictive narcotic cocaine works simply by dumping dopamine on the brain and preventing its re-uptake. In other words, dopamine creates a high—whether spurred naturally or artificially.

Oxytocin is a very different, but equally powerful, hormone. While dopamine is more individualistic in origin, oxytocin is relational. Oxytocin, which is often referred to as the 'trust or bonding hormone,' accounts for prosocial and antisocial behavior. As Sinek notes, oxytocin is what makes feelings of friendship or love possible. Oxytocin "is responsible for the warm and fuzzies." Sinek continues highlighting how oxytocin is what makes vulnerability, generosity, empathy, strong friendships, and, of course, love possible. It engenders human connectedness. The drive that you feel to help others and lend your skill and talents to them is the result of oxytocin. Without oxytocin, your passion would not be people-centered. While dopamine is more about instant gratification, Sinek suggests that oxytocin is about long-lasting bonds in noting how "the madness and excitement and spontaneity of the dopamine hit is replaced by a more relaxed, more stable, more long-term oxytocin-driven relationships."

Serotonin is, according to Sinek, "the feeling of pride we get when we perceive that others like or respect us. It makes us feel strong and confident, like we can take on anything." In fact, Sinek calls it the "leadership chemical" because it fuels us to seek the approval of others and raises our social status. Serotonin reinforces social bonding and a sense of accountability to those who offer us protection and support. As Sinek describes, "we can actually feel the weight of responsibility when others commit time and energy to support us. We want them to feel that the sacrifices they made for us were worth it. We don't want to let them down. We want to make them proud." The impactful role of serotonin is evident in Sinek's assertion that "whether we are a boss, coach or parent, serotonin is working to encourage us to serve those for whom we are directly responsible."

And, finally there are endorphins. Endorphins are simply about masking pain. Sinek aptly describes them as one's own personal opiate, often released in response to stress or fear. While endorphins are generally released during times of physical exertion—as in the very familiar example of the "runner's high"—they also come into play during the lightheartedness of laughter. As Sinek explains, "during tense times, a little lightheartedness may go a long way to help relax those around us and reduce tensions so that we can focus on getting our jobs done." This is a great reminder that in our pursuit of influence it is important not to take ourselves too seriously, and to allow infectious humor and laughter to ease our pain and the pain of others.

Hopefully, it is clear that the buzz you feel when you are pursuing your passion, interacting with those of similar interests, and helping those who benefit from your service is indeed biological. You were wired that way. The "selfish" chemicals of dopamine and endorphins push you toward your call while the "selfless" ones of oxytocin and serotonin keep you focused on others in the process. The Creator's genius in making us people who are wired to follow the sound of passion amazes me. Earlier, I described the etymology of the term "influence" as meaning "to flow into." With the advances of neurological imaging, we have not only developed a term "flow" that captures our optimal state of performance, but can also observe changes in our brain when in that flow state. Personally, I find it captivating to think that we are indeed performing optimally when we pursue the influence that our GODprint directs.

Simply put, the selfish chemicals encourage you, and the selfless chemicals help you encourage others. If you think of your dreams and purpose as a beacon towards which you run, then passion must be the homing device that directs you there. Inspired by your GODprint and your neurochemical cocktail, passion is that guiding force that keeps you on target. While GODprint is unique to each of us, passion is that unifying sound that connects—creating a bonding community. I love the way author George Bernard Shaw "insists that there are passions far more exciting than the physical ones . . . 'intellectual passion, mathematical passion, passion for discovery and exploration: the mightiest of all passions.'"[65] The goal here is to help discern passion's sound amidst the cacophony of noise in our daily routine. There are so many distractions with which to contend, especially for those of us on the second shift. The daily clamor includes day-job demands, household challenges, health distractions, and psychological fears—just to name a few. It is, frankly, disorienting. Fortunately, the dopamine-induced ability to focus allows us to listen with intent.

> Passion is designed to be a clarion call
> that constantly pulsates to guide
> your heart towards home.

---

[65] Encyclopedia, W.T.F. Passion (Emotion). [cited 2015].

I have an illustration to help solidify this principle. I have a pair of headphones that I typically use when traveling by airplane or when writing at my local Starbucks. These headphones are called noise-canceling, because they filter out sound at a certain decibel level. They do not block out all sound. But, they diminish the sound enough to allow me to focus on the task at hand. The sound of passion is much like this. Passion is designed to be a clarion call that constantly pulsates to guide your heart towards home. What do I mean by "home"? Home is that core sense of identity where you most come alive. In fact, my weekly podcast is called "The Leading You Home Podcast" because it focuses on helping individuals stay connected with those core values that define them and people who love them. Like those noise-canceling headphones, passion helps us stay goal-oriented and focused on our home by filtering out the distractions. The selfish chemicals of dopamine and endorphins are at work.

But, let me give you another example that demonstrates the social impact of oxytocin and serotonin. Imagine that you are sitting in your local Starbucks. As people come and go, there are noises all around you. For some, it can be distracting, but you are just hearing it and not really listening to it. None of it catches your attention. We know that attention is the necessary ingredient to convert hearing to listening, but your brain is not engaged with this banter because it does not trigger your antenna. Suddenly, however, while you are focused on your own project, you hear someone at an adjacent table make a comment about Star Trek, your favorite show of all time.

You have loved Star Trek for years. You have watched all of the episodes and know all of the characters. It catches your attention. You do not mean to eavesdrop, but you find yourself discreetly listening to what is being said. What are they saying about Captain James Kirk and Spock? It is a little hard to hear all of the details. But, your curiosity is piqued. Why? Because, when

143

you are conscious, your antenna of passion is constantly scanning your surroundings outside of your conscious awareness. When one of your triggers is introduced, your antenna alerts your consciousness and commands your attention. You have probably been in one of those situations where you have even tried to defocus on that trigger but you struggle to do so. Now that your attention is engaged, when appropriate to do so you may even introduce yourself and politely interject in the conversation. The group welcomes another "Trekkie." Over the next hour, the laughter and excitement creates an ephemeral buzz that feels like a reunion of old friends. The sound of passion is both personal and relational.

LISTENING IS LEARNING

Now that you understand the biology of the buzz, it is easy to see how encouragement is an action with amazing physiological benefits. Passion encourages influence. There is, however, one additional facet of the sound of passion that we must explore. That is expertise. When done in earnest, the sound of passion will always take you on a learning adventure. While passion is a necessary ingredient for ultimate influence, without expertise it often falls short of its full potential. Passion is most effectively demonstrated when it is laced with expertise. Most people, when they are passionate about a topic, want to learn more about it (at least initially). Passionate photographers aren't usually content to leave the camera on automatic settings. They want to develop expertise with the manual controls. Passionate writers attend writer's conferences and participate in writer's groups to develop their craft. Passionate athletes strive to develop greater skills at their sport. The sound of passion usually fosters a conviction to become more skillful or knowledgeable in its execution.

The challenge, however, is that many second shifters—out of fear, laziness, ignorance, or just lack of time—choose to resist passion's pull towards expertise. Given strained margins, developing expertise sometimes feels like a luxury that takes time away from our passionate pursuits. This, however, is short-term thinking. The reality is that if you are not continuously learning, you risk having your knowledge become outdated. You have to think of yourself as a reservoir of value. Your GODprint will push you to continually strive to offer value to others. And, you always want to offer value out of your abundance rather than scarcity. But, without a learning attitude that replenishes your reservoir, you can find yourself feeling depleted and of compromised value to your target audience.

Today, there really is little excuse to lack expertise in one's area of passion. With practically limitless resources available on the Internet, there is effectively no subject about which you cannot develop expertise. Websites such as Lynda.com and Udemy.com are just two examples of online repositories with literally thousands of courses for the inquisitive mind. Additionally, there are hundreds, if not thousands, of individuals with websites offering free content on your specific subject of interest. For example, on my own site, haroldarnold.com, I have hundreds of posts on building better relationships and leadership skills. I have learned the importance of leveraging technology to consume expertise and wisdom from those who I may never meet in person.

> The sound of passion will always lead
> you toward learning.

A wealth of information exists in blogs, podcasts, YouTube videos, and other social media channels that can teach you practically anything. If you have access to the Internet, a bounty of resources are available to you at little or no cost. Only initiative stands between you and expert status. And, to be clear, expert status does not mean that you know more on this topic than everyone else. Rather, it means that you know more on this topic than your target audience.

I am convinced that the sound of passion will always lead you towards learning. Earlier, I introduced you to my phrase that captures the benefit of maintaining a learning posture: "see more to know more to be more to live more to give more." That, in a nutshell, is the journey of influence. You need to take more in so that you can give more out—imagine that reservoir. I, like so many others, was waiting for that mentor to come that would take me under his or her wing and push me to higher heights. But, shortcuts are not good long-term solutions. You need to go through the learning process to fill your reservoir for sustained influence. And, in an era filled with noisy distractions, your sustained influence depends on your ability to learn faster.

In his book, *The Living Company: Habits for Survival in a Turbulent Business Environment*, Arie de Geus, long-time director of strategic planning for Royal Dutch Shell, deduced after closely studying twenty-seven large corporations that the secret to longevity was the ability to learn faster. That was it—the secret to centuries of thriving. According to de Geus, "The ability to learn faster than your competitors is the only sustainable competitive advantage."[66] While our passionate pursuit is not about outdoing the competition, it is about optimizing the reach of your voice. Research clearly shows that a persistent learning posture and filling your reservoir are critical components. As you move in the direction of your GODprint, your teachers will emerge. Just be open-minded and rebuke the DRAGONS' efforts to dismiss credible voices around you.

---

[66] Geus, A. D., *The Living Company: Habits for Surval in a Turbulent Business Environment*. 2002: Harvard Business Review Press.

You are wired to follow the sound of your own passion. When you do, at least five benefits accrue:

1) Focusing your life around a core identity and values,
2) Attracting people with similar passions who become your tribe,
3) Cultivating a sense of belonging and supportive community,
4) Breeding a learning culture, and
5) Fostering innovation and challenging conventional boundaries.

Ultimately, in my faith-based worldview, the sound of your passion and mine originate from a single sound, the voice of God calling us to relationship with Him and one another. As Jabez asked God, "'Oh that you would bless me and enlarge my border, and that your hand might be with me, and that you would keep me from harm so that it might not bring me pain!' And God granted what he asked" (1 Chronicles 4:10). Your obedience in following this clarion call will bless you and expand your territory.

CHAPTER 11

TRAIN YOUR EAR

"It takes a little bit of mindfulness and a little bit of attention to others to be a good listener, which helps cultivate emotional nurturing and engagement."

– DEEPAK CHOPRA

In the last chapter, I discussed the importance of keeping your passion antenna attuned to our environment so that you can feel and follow the buzz that makes you come alive. By following the sound of passion, you locate and stay true to your GODprint and to your tribe. That is the critical first step. Unfortunately, too many people err in thinking that this is the final step. It isn't.

Finding your tribe is one thing. Influencing them is another. But, influence them you must. In order to influence them, you must understand their needs and wants. You must appreciate and offer solutions to their pain points. You must be sensitive to the context and limitations they face. And, most importantly, you must appreciate your own biases and limitations. None of this happens without deliberate listening. This skill is being touted everywhere from the bedroom to the boardroom.

Regardless of the context, effective listening requires a trained ear. Hearing is innate and biological. Unless your ear is defective, you will hear. Listening, however, is psychological and is a learned skill. Relational mastery happens as you develop your ability to encourage through listening. Your ear, however, has to be trained to listen to God so your identity is clearer. Your ear has to also be trained to listen to your GODprint so that your voice is clearer. And, finally, your ear has to be trained to listen to those you serve so that your approach is clearer.

Since I was young, I have dabbled at the piano. My mom required that I take lessons when I was a kid (which I am very grateful for today). I played for my father's church until I left home for college. I knew how to read music. As much as I hoped I would, I never learned how to play without a music sheet. Through the years, I have admired those other musicians whose ears were so trained to the music that they could just pick the chords and ad lib. For years, I wished that I could do that. There is a term for this ability to play without the music sheet— "playing by ear." Some people have a natural gift that they develop. Others just practice it long enough to be good at it. Regardless, they have trained their ear to the sounds of each chord and note. Effective listening is much like this, too. Some people may be naturally better at it than others, but everyone can develop those listening skills. A trained ear is able to hear verbals and non-verbals. A trained ear is able to discern expressed and latent emotion. A trained ear recognizes its own biases and baggage. And, with these attributes, a trained ear is able to see and experience people and situations as they presently are—rather than what they were in the past or how you wish them to be in the future. It is evident then that when I talk about a "trained ear" this entails more than the two organs on the sides of your head.

> Listening is psychological and requires
> the full gamut of your senses.

As earlier noted, hearing is biological and only requires your ears. Listening is psychological and requires the full gamut of your senses. Listening requires attentiveness of the whole you. When you commit your whole self to listening, you will have many opportunities to influence and be influenced at home, in the community, and in the workplace.

As an example, a couple of years ago, Forbes contributor Meghan Casserly identified active listening (giving full attention to what other people are saying, taking time to understand the points being made, asking questions as appropriate, and not interrupting) among the ten skills that would get you hired.[67] We see that word "attention" again. In an earlier chapter, hearing expert Dr. Horowitz described it as the difference between hearing and listening. As you listen to your sound of passion, you are positioned to become the scratch to another's itch. There is, however, a major caveat. When paying attention, you have to differentiate between assumption and awareness.

Assumption is what in psychology is called a projection. This means that you interpret other's situations and motivations from your own point of view. The problem with assumption is that it can be wrong. You may not fully know all of the variables that are involved and thus jump to the wrong conclusion. You may be less familiar with a person than you think. You may have your own biases that distort the way that you see the situation. The reality is that we all make assumptions. There is certainly a

---

[67] Casserly, M., "*The 10 Skills that Will Get You Hired in 2013.*" 2012 [cited 2015 October 26 2015]; Available from: (http://www.forbes.com/sites/meghancasserly/2012/12/10/the-10-skills-that-will-get-you-a-job-in-2013/)

time and place where this is the most effective means of making progress. However, the bottom line is that being guided by one's assumptions in relationships frequently leads you to a wrong conclusion, and typically has a negative impact on those relationships in the process. Though arguably paying attention, if you are being guided by your assumptions you are not listening as well as the situation demands.

Awareness, however, is a different matter altogether. Awareness is sensitivity to what is happening in a situation. Awareness is reliance on your antenna of passion for discernment. Awareness demands full attention to the overt and covert facets of an interaction and situation. Awareness may sound simple, but it is complex because, when done well, it requires you to be in the present as much as possible, with minimal disruptions to your attention. This is listening at its apex. The challenge of the second shift is to make the most of your available time and resources by being super vigilant in your awareness or listening. I would argue, in fact, that second-shift success requires a listening culture. The trend towards a listening culture is increasingly evident, even in corporate America.

These are just some of the many benefits of training your ear:

- Provides ability to empathize with the struggles of your audience
- Provides ability to identify and relate the positivity (and beauty) in situations
- Heightens self-awareness, which minimizes the risk of destructive projections (transference and counter-transference)
- Facilitates understanding of shared experiences and points of individualization
- Breeds trust with your audience

THE MINDFULNESS MOVEMENT

In years past, pundits extolled the virtues of authoritarian style leaders such as Jack Welch (former CEO of GE), who practiced top-down management philosophies. These strategies assumed that people at the top of the organization had all the answers and were responsible for disseminating that knowledge down the organizational chart. In more recent years, leadership strategists have increasingly validated a bottom-up strategy that seeks and values the constructive input of people throughout the organization. Phrased another way, thriving organizations embrace an organic listening culture. More specifically, they are able to incorporate mindfulness as a corporate strategy.

So, what is mindfulness or mindful living? Mindfulness is a way of paying attention—in the present moment—to yourself, others, and the world around you. According to Professor Mark Williams of Oxford University, "Mindfulness is a translation of a word that simply means awareness."[68] Ann Mack, director of trendspotting at JWT, told the Huffington Post, "It's kind of a counter-trend to the past decade of overly stimulated, ADD-afflicted, tech-saturated culture that we've been living in. What was once the domain of the spiritual set has filtered into the mainstream as more people are drawn to this idea of shutting out distractions and focusing on the moment."[69]

As we focus on mindfulness in this chapter, keep this more familiar notion of awareness in your mind. The second-shift challenge is to listen attentively so as to be keenly aware of opportunities to share your passion. But, there is more. As we

---

[68] Mindfulnet: the mindfulness information website. 2011 [cited 2015]; Available from: http://www.mindfulnet.org/.
[69] Gregoire, C., "Why 2014 Will Be The Year Of Mindful Living." 2014 [cited 2015]; Available from: http://www.huffingtonpost.com/2014/01/02/will-2014-be-the-year-of-_0_n_4523975.html.

discussed earlier, second-shift success requires mastery of the margins of our lives and the ability to juggle many responsibilities. With so many things vying for your attention, most second shifters live constantly on the verge of overwhelm. And, of course, many influencers allow their passion fire to die because that burden overtakes them. Mindfulness is a part of the solution because it provides you with techniques to increase your psychological, emotional, and relational capacity.

Michael Chaskalson, the author of The Mindful Workplace and founder of Mindfulness Works Ltd, is one of the UK's leading mindfulness trainers. Chaskalson highlights studies at Harvard University and elsewhere, proving the sustained attention, emotional regulation, and perspective taking associated with mindfulness—which are associated with more happiness and well-being, and even better immune system functioning. Chaskalson explains that mindfulness gives insight into the emotions, increases attentiveness, helps regulate stress, minimizes mood disorders, and has a positive effect on physical problems like hypertension, heart disease, and chronic pain.[70]

While mindfulness has historically been niched in the Eastern spirituality movement, the reality is that the benefits of mindfulness are being widely acknowledged in corporate, educational, and home settings. According to J. Walter Thompson (JWT) Worldwide, one of the world's largest marketing communications brands, 2014 was projected to be characterized by a movement toward mindful living,[71] and

---

[70] Chaskalson, M., *The Mindful Workplace: Developing Resilient Individuals and Resonant Organizations with MBSR.* 2011: Wiley-Blackwell.
[71] Intelligence, J.W.T. "Get ready for the New Year – 100 Things to Watch in 2014." 2013 [cited 2015]; Available from: http://www.jwt.com/blog/consumer_insights/ready-for-the-new-year-100-things-to-watch-for-2014/.

mindful living was named one of ten trends that would shape the world in 2014 and beyond.[72]

Mindfulness isn't some passing fad sweeping middle management. Several studies have shown leader mindfulness was significantly associated with greater satisfaction and more favorable job performance ratings.[73] Corporate America has stood up and taken notice. For more than seven years, General Mills has been practicing mindfulness in the workplace and has been credited as transforming the culture of this Fortune 200 multinational. "It's about training our minds to be more focused, to see with clarity, to have spaciousness for creativity and to feel connected," says Janice Marturano, General Mills' deputy general counsel, who founded the General Mills mindfulness program.[74]

Silicon Valley may also be pioneering the mindfulness movement. As an example, Google "even offers its employees a program called Search Inside Yourself (SIY), a mindfulness-based emotional intelligence training program. Chade-Meng Tan, the program's founder and author of 'Search Inside Yourself,' highlights how mindfulness can help build compassion, which can be beneficial to not only individuals and community, but also to corporate bottom lines."[75] Even the US

---

[72] Worldwide, J.W.T. "10 Trends that Will Shape our World in 2014 and Beyond." 2013 [cited 2015]; Available from:
http://www.jwt.com/blog/consumer_insights/10-trends-that-will-shape-our-world-in-2014-and-beyond/.

[73] Jazaieri, H. "Can Mindful Managers Make Happier Employees?" 2014 [cited 2015]; Available from:
http://greatergood.berkeley.edu/article/item/can_mindful_managers_make_happier_employees.

[74] Gelles, D., "The mind business." 2012 [cited 2015]; Available from:
http://www.ft.com/cms/s/2/d9cb7940-ebea-11e1-985a-00144feab49a.html.

[75] Hochman, D., "Mindfulness: Getting Its Share of Attention." 2013 [cited 2015; Available from:

Military has gotten in on the mindfulness act, as "a study among U.S. Marines demonstrated that those trained in mindfulness experienced improved mood and working memory. Under pressure, they were more capable of complex thought and problem solving and they had better control of their emotions. Mindfulness training reduces the functional impairments associated with high-stress challenges that demand high levels of cognitive control, self-awareness, situational awareness and emotional regulation."[76]

BEING MINDFUL

We can see that mindfulness is already making substantive inroads in the corporate, and even military, context. Our goal, however, is to show its power to transform your listening posture. At its most basic, mindfulness is about listening to yourself, your environment, and those with whom you interact. "Some experts believe that mindfulness works, in part, by helping people to accept their experiences — including painful emotions — rather than react to them with aversion and avoidance."[77]

Over the course of more than twenty-five years on the day job in highly demanding fields, there have been moments when I have felt defeated. My emotions were frayed from very demanding projects, clients, and co-workers. My spirit was sullen from feeling as if I was not flourishing in the things that

---

http://www.nytimes.com/2013/11/03/fashion/mindfulness-and-meditation-are-capturing-attention.html.

[76] Reese, J., "Building Fit Minds Under Stress: Penn Neuroscientists Examine the Protective Effects of Mindfulness Training." 2010 [cited 2015]; Available from:
http://www.upenn.edu/pennnews/news/building-fit-minds-under-stress-penn-neuroscientists-examine-protective-effects-mindfulness-tra.

[77] Benefits of Mindfulness. [cited 2015]; Available from:
http://www.helpguide.org/harvard/benefits-of-mindfulness.htm.

mattered most to me. I remember those days, when I stood in the shower gasping for air because I was so overwhelmed with negative emotions. In those times, I felt like I had nothing left. My mind was flooded from what felt like a burden of life's past, present, and future disappointments. Fortunately, these periods for me have always been relatively short-lived. My personality does not allow me to dwell there — I am thankful for that. But, that does not diminish the feeling of futility when those episodes occur.

However, things changed for me after learning how to better control my thoughts — thanks to both mindfulness practices and the excellent attitude adjustment resources provided by Tony Robbins.[78] Both of these interventions' effectiveness centers on helping you think and live in what you can control in the present, rather than in the uncontrollable past or future. Mindfulness, at its most basic, is a meditative practice where one attends to one's breathing and focuses on whatever is happening in the present moment. But, mindfulness is also more intricate in empowering you to take a fresh look at the people and circumstances in your everyday lives. For example, one of the elements of mindfulness is called "attention reset." Simply put, it asks you to consider how, in any given situation, you would see and react to it if this was the first time you had ever encountered it. This practice alone transformed my experience on my day job. Practicing attention reset has required me to discount previous negative experiences with different individuals and see them from a different vantage point — in the present, the right now.

That, in fact, is the promise of mindfulness in general. With an intentional focus on one's current setting and experiencing people from a different point of view, we disrupt our brain from reverting to its conditioned pattern of response. That changes

---

[78] Robbins, A., *Personal Power II: The Driving Force*. 1996, Robbins Research International.

everything. I am not suggesting that it is easy to consistently stay in this mindset. It does take practice. But, when sustained, it literally creates new neural pathways in your brain—evidenced as more desirable habits.

> Active listening and being fully present really is a type of brain surgery.

With the metamorphosis that mindfulness causes in your brain, you can see that active listening and being fully present really is a type of brain surgery—though, thankfully, without the neurosurgeon. You and your cohort are transformed in this process of awareness and understanding. When you pay attention, the return on your investment is incalculable but the growth curve of your influence is undeniable.

CHAPTER 12

CRAFT YOUR VOICE

"One word expresses the pathway to greatness: voice. Those on this

path find their voice and inspire others to find theirs.

The rest never do."

—STEPHEN COVEY

It may seem a little odd to have a chapter about voice when we have been focused on listening. But, that is only because many fail to really understand the full meaning of one's voice. Your voice is not only the sound that comes from your mouth when you speak. Rather, your voice is the visible expression of your internal GODprint. In his book, *The 8th Habit: From Effectiveness to Greatness*, bestselling author Stephen Covey highlights voice as the catalyst for impact in today's influence economy. "Learn what taps your talents and fuels your passion—that rises out of a great need in the world that you feel drawn by conscience to meet—therein lies your voice, your calling, your soul's code."[79] Covey defines voice as "the

---

[79] Covey, S., *The 8th Habit: From Effectiveness to Greatness.* 2013: Simon and Schuster.

overlapping of the four parts of our nature: our body, our mind, our heart, and our spirit." Here is another way to think about it: Your voice gives legs to your purpose. Your voice is what people remember about you when you are no longer physically present.

> Voice is the unique way that each of us impacts the world around us.

Covey offers four questions to craft your voice in a way that honors your four-part nature:

1. What are you good at? (Mind)
2. What do you love doing? (Heart)
3. What need can you serve? (Body)
4. And finally, what is life asking of you? What gives your life meaning and purpose? What do you feel like you should be doing? In short, what is your conscience directing you to do? (Spirit)

Note how aligned Covey's model is with the notion of GODprint that we have adopted throughout this book. Voice is the unique way that each of us impacts the world around us. The volume and inflection in your voice are contingent on the intensity of your passion. We must address voice alongside listening, because we all have to attentively listen in order to calibrate our voice to the needs of those we are called to serve. Your voice is the conduit expressing your own sound of passion. Voice is something with which many would-be influencers struggle. I am included in that number. Before I explain that, let me use an example common in the context of the singing voice. Singers can sing in their full (or natural) voice. Many are also able to sing in falsetto. But, most singers are limited in how long they can stay in falsetto. It is unnatural for them.

This singing analogy also holds when you are giving voice to your GODprint. When you are "speaking" in your full and natural voice you are investing the best part of yourself. You are passing along your essence. Conversely, when you are trying to mimic another's voice you are in your falsetto. You may have some short-term impact. But, you will not sustain it because it is not naturally you. Yet, many of us get caught using our falsetto voice. It happens because we value the voice of those we perceive as achieving certain status more than we value our own voice. We essentially want to be a vocal impressionist. An impressionist is one whose act consists of imitating the voice of others and falling prey to the aforementioned copycat syndrome, rather than recognizing that you are a designer's original. We all fall into our falsetto at times. But, when you commit your energy to emulating others, rather than being true to yourself, you will always fall short of your life's purpose. Your destiny can only be credibly pursued in your full voice. But, like the pubescent teen, your voice may crack as it develops. That happens normally when you are exploring avenues of expression and interacting with others. Do not be alarmed. As you continue using your full voice, it will mature.

Even today, I struggle at times to stay in my full voice. My natural voice encourages people to pursue a life that gives their best self to benefit others and give honor to God. My voice empowers people to never settle for anything less than everything that God has for them. My voice is challenging — even for me. I struggle with my full voice because there are times when I question whether I have to just focus on pursuing God's best. Sometimes, I just want to talk in popular psychology terms that leave out specific reference to God so that I can be more liked by those outside of the faith community. I see other people of faith successfully do it. So, I go into falsetto voice. I become a copycat. I succumb to the shadow mission that I described back in Chapter 3. There is nothing wrong with having a voice that does not explicitly center on God's purpose. But, there is something wrong when my voice loses that focus because that is what God invested in me. That is my GODprint, my mission.

This chapter is about listening to your GODprint and crafting your authentic voice. The word "craft" is intentional here. To craft your voice is to intentionally develop and apply your GODprint in the shape of those who you are called to serve. Your voice has a range. There is not one tone or intensity that speaks to everyone. But, you can only modulate the tone and intensity of your voice as you follow the sound of passion and really listen to those in your sphere of influence. You may have a core message—most of us do. But, the style and delivery of that message is what makes it a craft. Your GODprint challenges you to craft your voice to serve those in your sphere of influence, in order that you might move them to a better state of being and, ultimately, toward what God created them to be. Your challenge is to craft a "winning voice."

A WINNING VOICE

In the Bible, the Apostle Paul provides what I believe is the best demonstration of crafting one's voice. It is summarized in 1 Corinthians 9:19–23, which reads: "Though I am free and belong to no one, I have made myself a slave to everyone, to win as many as possible. To the Jews I became like a Jew, to win the Jews. To those under the law I became like one under the law (though I myself am not under the law), so as to win those under the law. To those not having the law I became like one not having the law (though I am not free from God's law but am under Christ's law), so as to win those not having the law. To the weak I became weak, to win the weak. I have become all things to all people so that by all possible means I might save some. I do all this for the sake of the gospel, that I may share in its blessings" (NIV, emphasis added).

Paul followed his sound of passion across many cultures over the course of his two pivotal missionary journeys that exposed the known Gentile world to the gospel of Christ. His success is legendary and is still a model for modern missions. What made Paul the greatest Christian missionary in human history? Some might argue that it was his courage and conviction to preach the gospel. I certainly think that played a part. But, many courageous and convicted people are not successful in their endeavors. No. I believe that the Apostle Paul's success is outlined for us in this 1 Corinthians passage. I believe that this passage gives us a glimpse into Paul's GODprint. Paul's GODprint demonstrated a tenacity to win.

How do I know that this tenacity was a part of the Apostle Paul's GODprint? Well, scripture demonstrates it even before he was converted to Christianity. Prior to his Christian conversion, he was named Saul. He was a devout Hellenistic Jew and a Pharisee. And, Saul's reputation as a ringleader to make Christians extinct was widely known. He approached this task to extinguish Christianity with tenacity. "He did not want to merely contain Christianity or to drive it from Jerusalem; he wanted to rid the earth of Christianity and its followers. Thus, his opposition to Christ and His church took on a 'missionary' spirit."[80]

You can see that, even when he was Saul and diametrically opposed to the Christian message, his tenacity to win for his cause was undeniable. Saul had a supernatural encounter with God that completely transformed his allegiance from a persecutor to a proponent of the Christian church. After his conversion, Saul's name was changed to Paul. From that point forward, Paul's motivation to serve Christ was clear. Motivated

---

[80] Deffinbaugh, B., The Conversion of Saul (Acts 9:1-31). ACTS: CHRIST AT WORK THROUGH HIS CHURCH 2004 [cited 2015]; Available from: https://bible.org/seriespage/14-conversion-saul-acts-91-31.

by the Acts 1:8 admonition to bear witness to the gospel in "Jerusalem, and in all Judea and Samaria, and to the end of the earth," Paul's following of the sound of passion made him second only to Jesus Christ as the most intriguing figure of first-century Christianity. The Apostle Paul continued to follow that sound of passion until his beheading in Rome at the hands of Roman emperor Nero.

As we see in 1 Corinthian 9, Paul's motivation was to promulgate the gospel in winning people to Christ. His method was to craft his voice to, as he said, "become all things to all people." When amidst the Jews, Paul focused on the law. But, when speaking to Gentiles, he abandoned legalism. When working with those in a weakened state, he too took on a posture of weakness to identify with them. Paul identifies himself as a "slave to everyone." I think, however, it may be more appropriate to say that he was a slave to Christ. Interestingly, in the Book of Romans, Paul actually addresses his letter to the Roman church and identifies himself as "a slave of Christ Jesus, chosen by God to be an apostle and sent out to preach his Good News" (Romans 1:1, NLT). I surmise, then, that being a slave to Christ is, in fact, the same as being a slave to everyone that Christ calls you to influence. The term "slave" certainly has negative connotations in Western culture because of the history of oppression it connotes. In this biblical context, however, it is better understood as being a servant. A winning voice is one that seeks to serve first.

> You cannot have a one-size-fits-all mindset.

Your GODprint leads you to tailor your message based on who you need to serve. You cannot have a one-size-fits-all mindset. No. As discussed in earlier chapters, you need that open mindset that identifies with the nuanced needs of those you are called to serve. As we noted in the last chapter, your ears have to be trained to really listen to them. This listening posture then informs you how to craft your voice to best serve them.

When I taught parenting classes to homeless families, I had to craft my voice to empathize with the challenges associated with raising children well in the midst of unsettled and transitional surroundings. When I taught computer skills to women in crisis pregnancy centers, my voice needed to relate to the socioeconomic challenges and joblessness concerns that derailed so many of them. When I work with marital couples in crisis, my voice has to take a balanced appraisal of the stressors they face and their necessary resilience to overcome. When I am with my wife and children, my voice has to comfort and nurture who God designed them to be. The tone and intensity of my voice has to change commensurate with the situation, if I am to have my greatest impact. That, however, only happens when I am able to listen to them and discern the need.

FIVE STEPS TO VOICE CRAFTING

You have learned how to follow the sound of your passion to identify your community or tribe that resonates with your own GODprint. You have learned how to train your ear so that you can actively listen to God's direction and to the pain points and needs of those you are called to serve. But, ultimately, influence requires that you engage them in an encouraging way. The Apostle Paul was a master of this type of engagement because he favored flexibility over fixedness. You, too, can become all things to all people. This does not mean that you lose your core self. You must continually stay attuned to what God is doing in you, so that you do not lose that sense of personal identity. As we noted earlier, you have to stay focused on your WHY. The Apostle Paul's motivation was clearly articulated when he said, "I do it all for the sake of the gospel" (1 Corinthians 9:23).

Personally, my motivation is to see people aspire to who God created them to be—especially in their relationships. Are you able to as clearly state your own motivation?

> Crafting your voice is an act of service because it requires that you tailor your gift to the needs of others.

Effectively crafting your voice to serve those within your sphere of influence entails five interrelated steps that ultimately culminate the listening experience and create a sense of belonging.

1. Listen to Serve

People want to know that you can relate to their experience and their feelings. Would-be influencers often err in thinking that influence requires that one has all the right answers. Nothing could be further from the truth. People generally are much less interested in solutions than in service. I believe that we often err in focusing on giving solutions because that is often easier to do than to be a servant. Can you see the difference? Solutions are something that you give. Service is something that you demonstrate. Some people are full of theoretical answers to your problem. But, their lives often fail to demonstrate their advice. Serving, on the other hand, demands that you come alongside another person. It is putting your proverbial "skin in the game." It extends beyond speaking into doing. Serving is an investment.

Crafting your voice is an act of service because it requires that you tailor your gift to the needs of others. It challenges you to not become comfortable with one way of thinking. It pushes you to consider alternative ways to touch hard-to-reach populations. It asks that you leave your comfort zone and make yourself a servant to everyone in your path for the sake of the call.

2. Listen for Common Ground

The beauty of following the sound of your passion is that it places you in the company of similar others—those either with shared interests or who are in need of your gift. Another key benefit of listening and crafting your voice is to find a community of shared interests and needs. As you seek ways to engage your community, listen to their stories and tell similar ones from your own past. As you listen to their pains, share your own related hurts and the healing process you journeyed. The key is identification. By listening, you are able to craft your voice to show that you identify with the experiences of your community. They will value you as one of them. They will come to regard you as a trusted source because you "get" them. They are then ripe to receive your message. But, again, it also starts with listening to where they are.

3. Listen Inquisitively

One of the most underdeveloped skills among developing influencers is the ability to listen inquisitively. Being inquisitive means deepening the conversation through a series of related follow-up questions. People broadly enjoy the feeling that someone is interested in them and what they have to say. The problem, however, is that many people feel that no one actually cares about what they have to say. When you are inquisitive, you communicate otherwise. Inquisitive individuals stand out from the crowd because they exude care and depth in a culture that often feels needy and shallow. Standing out is a key skill in a noisy world where so many people sound the same. Odds are that they sound the same because they listen the same.

Inquisitive people ask questions that communicate their interest in the details. They ask the logical next question to strengthen engagement. The most helpful topic about which to inquire is pain points. With what is this person struggling? How did it feel to face that disappointment? Remember, you do not have to have the solutions. Being inquisitive communicates sincere interest to hear more.

4. Listen for Strengths

Another impactful way to craft a voice of influence is to affirm one's strengths. Everyone has strengths. Some are easy to identify. Others are more difficult. But, I have never met anyone for whom I could not identify some strength to encourage. Listening for strengths is important in a culture that saps people of their resilience. Many people feel defeated. They struggle with the confidence to do the right thing or to persevere through challenging times. They need someone to believe in them.

When you engage others, if you listen carefully you will be able to find something about which you can be positive. For a single mom who has made a string of bad decisions, you might affirm her dedication to her child. For the addict who just lost his family's entire savings, you might affirm how he never physically or verbally abused his wife or children. For the teen just released from juvenile detention, you might affirm his ability to serve his sentence without getting into more trouble. These are some of the more difficult cases. If you can find the strengths in these situations, you certainly can find them in less extreme examples.

By listening for strengths and then authentically reinforcing those strengths with people, you build their self-confidence. You help them see a grander vision of themselves. The reality is that often they will initially resist your efforts because they are so accustomed to defeatist thinking. Others have been so marginalized or ignored by trusted others that they cannot see themselves as having positive qualities. As we mentioned in earlier chapters, their sense of self categorizes them as all bad because of the mistakes they have made. Your challenge then is to break through the layers of self-deprecation so that their own GODprint can be reignited and allow them to see themselves how God sees them. Keep reinforcing their strengths until they internalize it for themselves. As you get through, you will become a trusted friend.

5. Listen Perpetually

The final component of listening is something I have found to have tremendous impact. It is the act of listening perpetually. In other words, how do you establish a pattern where you are always listening for a response? The answer is to continually extend the conversation. People typically end exchanges with a period. But, what if your important exchanges ended with different punctuation? How about a comma or dash that suggests there is more to come? Or maybe a question mark that expects a reply?

The point is that if you make a habit of extending the conversation, then you are inviting the other person to stay in dialogue with you. This practice alone will separate you from most influencers. People are not accustomed to engaging someone who keeps coming back for more. While some individuals will choose not to continue the conversation with you, many will.

You might be wondering how this looks practically. Let's say that someone asks you a question. Most people will just answer the question. But, what if, in addition to answering the question, you asked another in return? Avoid closed-ended questions (e.g., those starting with "Did" or "Do") that can be answered with a "yes" or "no" response. Instead, use open-ended questions (such as those starting with "How" or "Why") that can only be answered with narrative. It is like a tennis match where you always commit to return the ball to the other person's court. If it is a person who you are called to influence, do not let the ball drop on your side of the court. Hit it back.

Of course, there are some conversations that you do not want to extend. In these cases, it is perfectly legitimate to simply respond and let the conversation terminate. But, when following the sound of your passion, you are going to encounter many individuals with whom you need to extend the conversation perpetually. It is not always easy to think of a creative way to return the ball to their court. It might take a little research or craftiness on your side because you do not want to be perceived as a nuisance. Hence, you have to consider creative ways to express an idea. This style of listening will help you craft your voice to elicit deeper levels of engagement.

LISTENING QUESTIONS

In Chapter 11, I suggested that attention separates hearing from listening. As I close this critical section on listening, I would like to offer you five questions that I have found most advantageous to really demonstrate attentive listening. These questions, when asked in the spirit of encouragement, foster a sense of empathic understanding. For each question, I have included what the goal of that question is in order to contextualize it for you.

Question #1: How does this situation make you feel?

Goal: The key to this question is emotional expression— which is hard for many people. When asked, it communicates to the other party that what is going on inside of them is important to you. Even though you may not be able to identify with the

169

details of their situation, your goal in asking the question is to identify with the emotion they feel. In other words, if the other person feels "lonely," then think to yourself when you felt isolated or lonely. This will help you empathize with what the other person is feeling.

Question #2: How can I help or encourage you through this situation?

Goal: This question shows your willingness to make this person's problem your own problem. Even if there is nothing that you can tactically do to help, it sends an important message to the other person that you are walking alongside them. Asking this question also helps overcome some gender differences. Men often want to be fixers while women often just want a caring listener. So, this helps to understand what the person really needs from you.

Question #3: How, if at all, have I disappointed you in this situation?

Goal: Disappointment is a fact of life. Sometimes, people are disappointed in us and we don't even realize it—at least the magnitude of it. This question shows that you are open to accepting your own responsibility, if any, in the situation. The other person will respect you for this openness.

Question #4: What can we do differently next time?

Goal: This question is forward looking. It acknowledges the past while challenging the other party to consider what steps can be done now to try for a more desirable outcome.

If you are a person of faith, you can also include this fifth question that acknowledges a more transcendent force at play.

Question #5: How can I pray for you?

Goal: This question places a priority on spiritual intercession. It says this situation is bigger than you and me.

All of your situations may not warrant asking all five questions. But, carefully consider the situation and choose any or all of them that you think might help. Remember that your goal is to objectively and attentively listen to the response. Do not feel compelled to offer an answer or a solution. Just listen. Also, if applicable, do not try to defend yourself as you listen. The speaker will eventually feel safer sharing with you if s/he believes that you can actually hear non-defensively.

PART 4:

THE LOVE OF INFLUENCE

CHAPTER 13

LOVE FOR BELONGING

"The first duty of love is to listen."

—PAUL TILLICH

Theologian Paul Tillich's famous expression about love is the perfect segue from our listening emphasis to the next leg of framework.[81] We now turn our attention to the imperative to love. But, we can only do so as we appreciate that love is only possible in a listening culture. In previous chapters, the importance of listening was extolled in order to discover your passion and your tribe. Listening can put you in a position of influence if you are willing to craft your voice to meet the needs of those in your path. But, listening is not the end goal. Listening is the compass that points you in the right direction—always towards your GODprint.

The next several chapters, however, offer you guidance on how to demonstrate godly influence as you walk your path. As Tillich notes, listening is indeed the first duty of love. Our focus now shifts to love. Godly influence, in fact, only happens in the

---

[81] Tillich, P., *Love, Power, and Justice: Ontological Analyses and Ethical Applications.* 1960: Oxford University Press.

context of love. Those of us in the Christian tradition know that our faith centers on love. When asked what is the greatest commandment, Jesus unequivocally responds that love for God and for people is the highest aspiration:

> "Teacher, which is the great commandment in the Law?" And he said to him, "You shall love the Lord your God with all your heart and with all your soul and with all your mind. This is the great and first commandment. And a second is like it: You shall love your neighbor as yourself. On these two commandments depend all the Law and the Prophets." (Matthew 22:36–40)

There is nothing more important. Listening is a necessary but insufficient ingredient. It takes love to truly transform your life and those to whom you are called to serve. Love is the second leg in the three-legged stool of influence.

The word *love* is a multi-faceted term. Western culture has historically approached love from a romantic, familial, or ministerial perspective. For most of us, love most immediately invokes images of intimacy, whether of couples or between parents and their children. But, we need to consider love from a more comprehensive perspective. Love is a relational investment, regardless of the setting. Love builds relational equity by investing the best of yourself to develop the best of someone else. In his book, *On Caring,* author Milton Mayeroff affirms the investment nature of love in defining love as the selfless promotion of the growth of the other.[82] Love is an emotion. But, more importantly, love is an action. Jesus communicates this in stating, "Little children, let us not love in

---

[82] Mayeroff, M., *On Caring.* 1990: William Morrow Paperbacks.

word or talk but in deed and in truth" (1 John 3:18). Love is far more about what you do than what you say.

> When you become love, it represents
> a core value of who you are.

While some might say the next three chapters are about showing love, I would reframe this assertion. The next several chapters are about becoming loving. Many excellent books have been penned on how to show love. But, much fewer have inspired us how to be love. Is there a difference between showing love and being love? I think so. When we show love, it is specific to a time and place. In other words, you can show love to one person but not to another. You might demonstrate love today. But, tomorrow may be a different story. However, when you become love, it represents a core value of who you are. Regardless of the situation or people that you face, you maintain an attitude of love. It is the nature of your character. Psychologist Carl Jung captured it well when he said, "I am not what has happened to me. I am what I choose to become."[83] And, as Tim Sanders wrote in his hugely popular book, *Love is the Killer App: How to Win Business and Influence Friends,* love is as important in the workplace as it is in the home.[84] It makes sense when you remember that love is something you become.

Love starts inwardly and—like a river—flows outwardly. Christian theologians, from St. Augustine in the fourth century to the Protestant Reformation's Martin Luther in the sixteenth century, have critically opined that the whole of scripture is inspired to instruct us how to love either God or our neighbor.

---

[83] Eckl, C. *What is the Meaning of Meaning?* 2011 [cited 2015]; Available from: https://www.psychologytoday.com/blog/beautiful-grief/201110/what-is-the-meaning-meaning.
[84] Sanders, T., *Love Is the Killer App: How to Win Business and Influence Friends.* 2002: Crown Business.

You can never truly love others unless you first love yourself. Similarly, you can never love yourself if you do not love your GODprint—what God put in you. And, ultimately, you can never love your GODprint or your purpose without loving the God that made that investment in you.

Scripture tells us that love—for God and for one another—is the greatest commandment. For years, I have always thought of these as two separate admonitions. But, as my understanding grows, I can see that these are actually on the same love continuum. I believe that is why Christ gave them equal importance. You simply cannot love God without loving others. Conversely, you cannot genuinely love others without loving God. They are two sides of the same coin, as elegantly captured in the poignant line from the French musical, Les Misérables, "To love another person is to see the face of God."[85]

> When you become love, you find love for people . . . even when they do not deserve it.

Over the next three chapters, we will explore what it means to become love. When you become love, you find the love in what you do—rather than waiting for the panacea to arrive. When you become love, you find love for people . . . even when they do not deserve it. When you become love, you see yourself the way that God sees you—as a dim reflection of his image. Becoming love is a key step in the second-shift journey because it seems that, more often than not, we are working in situations that are less than ideal. We frequently struggle to have our ducks lined up just as we would like them. We are often sitting by the phone or email inbox, waiting for that break to come. The challenge to become love means that we live out the words of the Apostle Paul to be content in whatever circumstances we

---

[85] Hugo, V., *Les Misérables*. 2013: Signet.

find ourselves when stating, "Not that I am speaking of being in need, for I have learned in whatever situation I am to be content" (Philippians 4:11).

> To fully love God is to fully trust that all things are working together for my good as I walk in obedience to him.

While I appreciate the admonition of Jung, I am still working on becoming love. It is difficult to sustain because it requires trust. For many years, I have struggled to feel content on my first shift as I yearn to pursue my passions full-time. I have moments when I feel the twinge of disappointment as my email distribution list grows at what seems like a snail's pace or my blog posts garner few comments. I can easily slip into feeling irrelevant. Do you see how quickly the shift can occur from a statement of what we do to a statement about who we are? This is when you know it is the DRAGONS rearing their ugly head. This discontent, of course, stems from my struggle to fully love God. To fully love God is to fully trust that all things are working together for my good as I walk in obedience to him. The reality, of course, is that I can never be irrelevant to God, regardless of how much social proof I accrue.

As with listening, the next three chapters examine three love hacks that are necessary to live out the greatest commandment to love God and your neighbor.

Loving Practice #1: *Empower Weakness*—this practice challenges you to use vulnerability to esteem yourself and combat the shame that cripples those you are called to influence.

Loving Practice #2: *Grow Small*—this practice encourages you to a posture of humility that earns the trust of others and positions you for kingdom living.

Loving Practice #3: *Accumulate Generosity*—this practice affirms the work of others and engenders reciprocity necessary to sustain communities of encouragement.

CHAPTER 14:

EMPOWER WEAKNESS

"I had no idea that being my authentic self could make me as rich as

I've become. If I had, I'd have done it a lot earlier."

—OPRAH WINFREY

Love begins with authenticity. There can be no other way. Authenticity asks what you were born to do and then holds you accountable for spending your lifetime chasing that birthright. Two biblical passages capture the design of authenticity. The first is Psalm 139:14, which tells each of us that we are "fearfully and wonderfully made." The word *wonderfully* means to be distinct or unique. Then consider Ephesians 2:10: "For we are God's masterpiece. He has created us anew in Christ Jesus, so we can do the good things he planned for us long ago" (NLT). Combining these two passages, we surmise that you are a one-of-a-kind masterpiece, created to follow the sound of passion and do good things in the process. Love begins with authenticity because the first place to experience love is to feel it within and feel secure in your own skin. Authenticity is what makes you uniquely you. Authenticity is what allows you to wield influence in places inaccessible to everyone else. Authenticity is a magnetic force that draws people towards you. When you are most authentic, you should be at the pinnacle of joy with a radiance that brightens everyone around you

I have talked about authenticity's benefits. But, what exactly does authenticity look like? At its simplest, authenticity is to be genuinely comfortable and confident with who you are at your core. In her book, *The Gifts of Imperfection: Letting Go of Who You Think You Are Supposed to Be and Embrace Who You Are*, Dr. Brene Brown addresses the concept of wholehearted living, which she defines as "engaging our lives from a place of worthiness. It means cultivating the courage, compassion, and connection to wake up in the morning and think, 'No matter what gets done and how much is left undone. I am enough.' It's going to bed at night thinking, 'Yes, I am imperfect and vulnerable and sometimes afraid, but that doesn't change the truth that I am also brave and worthy of love and belonging.'"[86]

I am convinced that wholehearted living is the lifestyle to which God calls us. From her bevy of research on this topic of wholehearted living, Dr. Brown concludes one of its ten central tenets is the ability to cultivate authenticity—which means releasing yourself from the burden of what other people think and making daily choices that align with your GODprint. Dr. Brown continues to describe that, "authenticity is a collection of choices that we have to make every day. It's about the choice to show up and be real. The choice to be honest. The choice to let our true selves be seen."[87] That applies not only to the way others see us, but also to how we see ourselves.

> Authenticity in this purest form is to be fully in tune with one's own nature and deftly exude this nature in one's environment

---

[86] Brown, B., *The Gifts of Imperfection: Let Go of Who You Think You're Supposed to Be and Embrace Who You Are.* 2010: Hazelden.
[87] Ibid, pg. 49.

Many, however, think about authenticity in the binary sense, as something that you either are or are not. I do not think this is the most helpful way to look at it. It is more accurate to think about authenticity on a scale from zero to one-hundred percent authentic. When one is living without any sense of authenticity, he is in full denial of who he is as a person, the nature of his gifts, and the reason for his existence. I see few people that are so profoundly deluded. Most people exhibit at least a semblance of authenticity. I also believe few, if any, people are one-hundred percent authentic. Pure authenticity will always be aspirational because, as E. E. Cummings notes, "to be nobody-but-yourself in a world which is doing its best, night and day, to make you everybody but yourself—means to fight the hardest battle which any human can fight—and never stop fighting."[88] Authenticity in this purest form is to be fully in tune with one's own nature and deftly exude this nature in one's environment in a way that helps other people discover themselves and God.

WHOLEHEARTEDLY AUTHENTIC

Being wholeheartedly authentic means making choices consistent with your GODprint. When operating authentically, you recognize the value of your gifts, both natural and acquired, that make you come alive. When wielded with authenticity, these gifts are the tools that facilitate your creativity as a builder, advocate, aesthetic, or networker as described in more detail in Chapter 8. Authentic gifts have that effect because they connect you to other people.

Given all that authenticity promises, why is it so elusive? Well, the problem, of course, is that authenticity requires that we face the negative aspects of ourselves and experiences, too. These are often the shameful incidents that we do not want

---

[88] Cummings, E. E., *E.E. Cummings, a miscellany*. 1958: Argophile Press.

anyone to know. We have built defense mechanisms to protect us from the emotional tumult. Authenticity is one of the buzzwords in culture today, but really living it out can be one of the scariest things you ever face. Authentic living can be a very difficult and painful experience, particularly for those who have been physically or emotionally victimized.

The promise, however, of wholehearted authenticity is that it acknowledges those imperfections, fears, and defense mechanisms. Wholehearted authenticity demands that we face those hurtful situations from a healing perspective, rather than attempt to bury them. Recently, I explained to a group of leaders that I take the approach of exposing practically any of the mistakes of my past if I believe that it will help someone. This practice feels redemptive for me. As I share about my missteps and moments that could be embarrassing, I honestly feel a cleansing process taking place. I actually look forward to sharing my pains because, somehow, giving it as an encouragement for others redeems the negativity of the experience to me. The more I tell it, the less power it has over me. For me, that is the face and power of vulnerability.

The key to balancing the ebbs and flows of wholehearted authenticity is best summed in the notion of vulnerability. As captured in her 2010 TedX Houston talk, "The power of vulnerability" (which has reached viral proportions online), Dr. Brown explains vulnerability as "uncertainty, risk, and emotional exposure."[89] Most of us exert enormous effort to minimize our vulnerabilities because they are socially stigmatized as signs of weakness. Hence, we resist the idea of being overexposed. The irony, however, is that, as Dr. Brown suggests, the richer experiences of life such as "love, belonging, trust, joy, and creativity" all require vulnerability. Hence, to

---

[89] TED. Brene Brown: *The Power of Vulnerability*. 2010 [cited 2015]; Available from:
https://www.ted.com/talks/brene_brown_on_vulnerability.

guard yourself from being vulnerable is to inhibit your ability to connect in deep, life-giving relationships. Following your sound of passion will always lead you to a place of vulnerability. You then must decide how much of yourself you will commit to your passion. Remember that passion is demonstrated as your "Pass-I-On." That "I" is your wholehearted self.

In a recent interview that I had with master copywriter, author, and entrepreneur Ray Edwards on my Leading You Home Podcast, we discussed this issue of vulnerability. I was struck by his admonition to the budding or experienced platform builder that the place to focus to wield influence is usually the place that makes you most uncomfortable. Edwards notes that, in his experience, people get a sense that you're being real when you go to those places where you feel the most vulnerable and experience the most fear about what people will think and what their reaction will be. That place of uncertainty is also the place of healing. Uncertainty is a scary place for most of us. But, it offers yet another example of the way in which your destiny is reached outside of your comfort zone. Ray Edwards gives his own example of a vulnerability for him as he talks about his health battles:

"Some time ago I let some information go about my health. I went public with what a lot of people in my position want to conceal—any perceived weaknesses or vulnerabilities. I just felt really strongly that I'm dealing with something called Parkinson's Disease. I felt strongly that I had some answers for people about how to face things like this that if I didn't share them that I wasn't really being a good steward of what I've been given. I certainly don't think the disease is a gift that I've been given. But, I do think the ability to respond to it from a God perspective is a gift that I've been given. So, to not share that with people would be robbing them of something that God has entrusted to me."[90]

WEAKNESS AS A LOVE HACK

The Apostle Paul models the power of vulnerability in his second letter to the Corinthian church as he writes about the struggle with his own weakness, which he describes as a "thorn in his flesh." He repeatedly asks God to remove this torment from him. But, God's response is unyielding: "My grace is sufficient for you, for my power is made perfect in weakness" (2 Corinthians 12:9). Despite Paul's pleas, God desires to show his perfect power through Paul's vulnerability. This, of course, speaks volumes to us as well.

Upon considering God's reply, Paul makes the choice to tout his vulnerabilities even more forcefully so that God's power is indeed manifest through him. Paul says it this way: "Therefore I will boast all the more gladly of my weaknesses, so that Christ's power may rest upon me. For the sake of Christ, then, I am content with weaknesses, insults, hardships, persecution, and calamities. For when I am weak, then I am strong" (2 Corinthians 12:9-10). Lest you think this was just a passing thought for Paul, he reiterates the point in an earlier verse: "If I must boast, I will boast of the things that show my weakness" (2 Corinthians 11:30).

As I consider Paul's words, I better understand why I feel purified as I share my own failings with others. I see why Ray Edwards believes his ability to respond to his diagnosis of Parkinson's Disease from a godly perspective is a gift from God. These vulnerabilities and weaknesses are not negative at all—at least not when they are submitted to God. They are strengths.

---

[90] Arnold, H., The Leading You Home Podcast, in LYH51: Where Business Meets Ministry. 2015: HaroldArnold.com.

Yes, they are painful, inconvenient, and troubling. But, God promises to give you sufficient grace to endure it so that it can demonstrate his perfect power. Though Dr. Brown's research on vulnerability gives a contemporary lens and dataset to understand the power of authenticity, the Apostle Paul penned a central truth more than two thousand years ago—"When I am weak, then I am strong." When properly contextualized, weakness is not weak at all. Weakness is a love hack—"a tip or efficient method for showing love."[91]

I previously described the Apostle Paul's uncanny ability to be all things to all people. He followed the sound of his passion on two historic missionary journeys. He is inarguably the greatest Christian missionary in history. But, what made him so adaptable in his efforts to win people to Christ? I believe it was his wholehearted authenticity. Despite his own struggles and weaknesses, he maintained a core sense of his identity. In other words, because he could stay grounded in who God said he was, he could demonstrate flexibility in his ministry. His shortcomings empowered him to rely on God's provision and grace. His weakness showed God's grace and love to him and those to whom he ministered the gospel.

As a second shifter, Paul's flexibility is equally imperative to demonstrate love to your tribe in your own pursuit of influence. Constantly reinventing yourself is a demonstration of your love for your tribe. When you do it as a means of being true to your GODprint, you bring honor to God through your efforts. You, too, have to be confident in yourself in order to be able to be all things to all people without losing the true you.

Pursuing your influence in the margin of your life often exposes your weaknesses. For some, it's fear of failure, poor time-management skills, or self-limiting beliefs inspired by the

---

[91] Dictionary.com, "Hack." Available from:
http://dictionary.reference.com/browse/hack?s=t.

DRAGONS. For others, it may be health, family, or work challenges that consume what little energy you have left. Still others may see character and spiritual weaknesses emerge. We all have our weaknesses. But, what you do with your weaknesses determines their effectiveness as your love hack. Will you give that weakness to God as an offering for healing, or allow it to fill you with shame, avoidance, and deceit? It isn't what happens to you that demonstrates your love for God, yourself, your passion, and others. Rather, hacking love lies in your response to what happens to you. God's power is made perfect in your weakness.

> Weakness is a game changer because it can position you to completely surrender yourself to God as your advocate.

Weakness is so effective as a love hack because it reduces your self-reliance and attunes you to forces outside yourself. Weakness can put you at the end of your perceived self-sufficiency. Weakness helps you release your illusions of control as you see your own frailties and maladaptive patterns. Weakness challenges your presumptions and pushes you to dig for deeper reservoirs of strength. Because of its negative social stigma, weakness can push you towards God, the one reliable, perpetual source of strength and trustworthiness. Weakness is a game changer because it can position you to completely surrender yourself to God as your advocate.

> You become love when you become authentically weak and vulnerable.

The message here is this: to empower rather than to deny weakness is to hack love. It is a countercultural message that was promoted by Jesus Christ himself. Empowering weakness shifts your faith from self-directed to God-directed. Empowering weakness allows you to integrate the fragile and resilient parts of yourself into wholehearted engagement with God, yourself, and others. This is the countercultural message of love. You become love when you become authentically weak and vulnerable. Yes, it can be fraught with trepidation. We are human, after all. But, you have to remember the source of our strength. Your strength is God's grace. Your weakness allows God's grace to flourish. The Apostle Paul was clearly motivated by his desire that Christ's power be exemplified in his life. Christ's power is the central point here. You cannot empower weakness under your own strength—pride gets in the way. Left to your own devices, you will only extol and value your own strengths. But, authentic weakness unleashes Christ's power in your life—which does have the ability to empower your shortcomings.

Paul's result speaks for itself. His pursuit of influence transformed the face of Christianity by taking the gospel to the Gentile nations of the world. His feat is particularly impressive when we consider that the early Christian church was originally Jewish. Prior to Paul's transformation, the apostles focused their preaching to the Jews—their own familiar nationality. Paul was a Jew as well. But, as he followed the sound of his passion, it led him to foreign lands among people of different faiths and cultures, where he encountered all manner of ungodly practices. In places such as Corinth, he focused on warning against sexual immorality. When addressing the young church of Colosse, he admonished them against gnosticism that led them to believe that they could essentially follow their own desires and impulses. The point is that Paul's passion was to spread the gospel, regardless of the cultural constraints he faced.

In the Book of Galatians, we see that Paul had a profound sense of his GODprint as he wrote, "But when he who had set me apart before I was born, and who called me by his grace, was pleased to reveal his Son to me, in order that I might preach him among the Gentiles, I did not immediately consult with anyone" (Galatians 1:15-16). Paul did not seek permission from anyone because he understood his own GODprint to spread Christ's love beyond the Jewish community. With the same conviction that he had persecuted the Christian church, Paul became its greatest ambassador. That is Paul's love story, but yours is no less important. When you allow Christ to empower your weakness, you rise in strength. As you do so, you are in a position to encourage others to do the same.

CHAPTER 15

GROW SMALL

"It was pride that changed angels into devils; it is humility that makes

men as angels."

– SAINT AUGUSTINE

In the previous chapter, we examined the importance of authenticity and vulnerability to demonstrate love for God, yourself, and others. It is the critical step in building relationships and influence on any shift. However, it is particularly germane on the second shift, which is often fraught with the frustration of passion that feels marginalized. Sometimes, you just feel like a failure because things have not gone as you expected. We begin to question whether we are just an imposter. I know the feeling well. But, I have also come to understand the nature of the DRAGONS. And, that helps me to recognize the self-doubt for what it is, rather than an indictment of my capability. When I see the DRAGONS for what they are, I also see my ability (as Ray Edwards said in the previous chapter) to leverage my vulnerabilities as a gift. But, authenticity alone is not love. It is only love's enabler. The next step on this journey to become love is to adjust your posture.

Let's take a closer look at this notion of posture. Posture, in this context, and as presented in the dictionary, is "a mental or spiritual attitude."[92] But, for a moment, let's use our physical posture to illustrate a concept. A couple of years ago, I made my first visit to a chiropractor. The chiropractor pointed out several ways in which I exhibit poor posture. He not only associated some minor symptoms (e.g., fatigue, muscle tightness) that I currently experience to poor posture, but he also said that (if not corrected), over time, my poor posture may result in more serious health problems. The challenge, of course, is that my poor posture has been years in the making. It is mostly subconscious and not easy to change. But, I have to make a consistent and conscious effort to have proper posture if I want my physical body to function the way that God designed it to. We need to focus not only on physical posture, but also spiritual posture. Jesus describes this type of posture as follows in the Book of Matthew: "Truly I say to you, unless you turn and become like little children, you will never enter the kingdom of heaven"(18:3).

What does scripture mean to suggest that heaven will only be gained for those who become like little children? I believe it is a profound statement not of stature but of attitude—our attitudinal posture. None of us can sustain the direction or health that God desires for our relationships if we have a poor mental or spiritual attitude. Over time, it is typically poor posture that causes those good intentions of ours to go awry. Like the chiropractor teaching me to improve my posture through proper shoulder and head placement, God's formula for improved posture is captured in Matthew 18:3. Let's take a closer look at the context in which Jesus offered this admonition. The disciples were having a debate about who was to be the greatest in the kingdom of heaven. Their debate was ostensibly about

---

[92] Dictionary.com, "Posture." Available from:
http://dictionary.reference.com/browse/posture?s=t.

power, prestige, and reward. With one sentence, Jesus flipped their whole notion of power and influence upside down.

Herein lies the amazing paradox which forms the foundation of successful relationships. What Jesus sternly conveys, particularly for those in pursuit of great things (including great relationships), is that real success can only be achieved through smallness—not of stature (as symbolized by the child) but of posture. But, that sounds strange. Isn't bigger better? That is what secular culture teaches us. But, not when we speak of the posture God desires of us. Clearly, Jesus is teaching a counter-cultural truth—the opposite of what our culture rewards. For those seeking God's kingdom, the message is clear. Grow small—an oxymoron for sure.

Growing small is a hard concept to embrace because it conflicts with tendencies toward self-interest and promotion. This, of course, is why the disciples were trying to figure out how to out-jockey one another to be seen as great in Jesus' eyes. In his commentary on this Matthew passage, Dr. Knox Chamblin notes this passage as conveying that "one may be a disciple in pretense or in truth."[93] And he goes on to describe how Jesus expects true disciples (including you and me) to display a particular character and adopt a particular pattern of conduct. Following the direction and maintaining posture that the Lord expects is a process of relational and spiritual maturity. As such, we are at our best as we learn to develop a small posture in all of the relationships that God holds us responsible to steward. This, too, is the process of becoming love.

The message here is that life surrounds you with difficult circumstances that can test your relationships with your family members, some of whom may seem unappreciative, incommunicative, and disrespectful of you. The workplace frustrates you with tangled webs of relational distrust where

---

[93] Chamblin, K., Commentary on Matthew 18:1-14.

everyone fends for his or her own self-interest and promotion. Even friends and fellow church members who you hoped to lean on through troubling situations often leave you feeling alone to find your own way. You wonder why is this happening. Is it possible that your well-meaning intentions are disappointing because your posture in your relationships lacks kingdom-focus?

GROWING SMALL AT HOME

While some intuitively grasp what it means to grow small, others may struggle to discern its practical application. In my training and experience as a relationship educator, here are some real-life examples of demonstrations of growing small.

An Atlanta-area pastor and mentor of mine once took a leave of absence from work, despite the personal and financial consequences, to stay consistently by his wife's side in prayer until she was healed from the cancer that had stricken her body. God honored his smallness in her healing.

I was speaking with a group of couples about the premises around growing small in marriage. One of the wives astutely commented, "I know that we are talking about marriage. But, what is really convicting me right now is how this informs my interaction with my children." She is exactly right. Often in our parent-child relationships, we parents deliberately exert our power over our children to convince them to behave in a desirable manner. Obviously, this is often a necessary and expected component of parenting. The point, however, is that there are times when effective parenting necessitates that we grow small in our posture to get on the level of our children in order to best relate and motivate them. Some parents are leery to do this, for fear of losing their parental authority. The reality, however, is that (when done responsibly) growing small towards our children enhances our communication with them, which in turn creates the possibility for a better bonding experience. And, this does not just apply to small children.

I am reminded of a time when my then 20-year-old son had gotten himself into some trouble that was extremely hurtful to our family. I was so angry with him that I had a hard time feeling emotionally connected to him. But, I became convicted with my posture, and went to him to sincerely apologize for my emotional distancing. I assured him that I would be with him through the thick and thin of the incident. I did not condone what my son did; however, my ability to grow small brought us much closer together, even to this day. Growing small in our marriages, our parenting, and other family relationships allows us to be a beacon of God's light that interrupts the relational darkness that often fractures families.

Fractured families are an all-too-common byproduct of individuals who resist growing small. My wife and I recently experienced a stark example of the relational melee that can persist when this happens to a couple. A clear example of a marriage in need of smallness is that of Charlie and Susan (names have been changed). Though both Charlie and Susan individually are wonderful people, their marriage—already once separated—seems to stay perpetually teetering on the brink of another separation, or possibly divorce. Despite their devout Christian faith, the presence of children, and even their leadership role in their church's marriage ministry, this couple's relationship is lost in a complex maze of mutual distrust, blame, and disrespect. Through our honest conversation, it became clear that both the husband and wife feel exasperated and—to some degree—trapped. Fortunately, they have not lost all hope yet. But, each of them, tired from the years of emotional frustration, is steadily losing the will to believe that their marriage can ever recover, much less find that treasure of wholehearted love.

GROWING SMALL AT WORK

For others, God challenges us to grow small in our workplace. Most of us spend the majority of our waking hours at work, often surrounded by people from a variety of backgrounds, belief systems, and life challenges. From an early age, I have had a profound sense that God places us in our respective jobs to be witnesses for him—both by performing our jobs with technical excellence and by cultivating positive relationships. Over the years, I have worked countless hours beyond quitting time to complete my job responsibilities, because I had taken the time during normal business hours to listen and share hope to a co-worker in need of an understanding friend. The workplace presents a number of opportunities for growing small.

For example, growing small can be accomplished through your ability to stay centered when those around you are in flux, when you allow a colleague to get the credit rather than seek glory for yourself, when others see you as a safe haven to share their life concerns, and when you refuse to compromise ethics despite pressure. Yes, growing small at work is often fraught with political, and possibly even financial, consequences. But, there is no question that God honors these acts in his own system of acceptance and promotion.

I appreciate the words of Tim Sanders in *Love is the Killer App*, when he points out our obligation to create more value in our workplace than the salary that we are paid by intelligently and sensibly sharing our knowledge, network, and compassion. We all have to add value rather than be a "value vampire." He notes, "The value with you inside a situation is greater than the value without you." This posture prioritizes the good of the workplace over one's own feeling of the moment. Growing small at work is, according to Sanders, "the lovecat way."[94]

GROWING SMALL IN MINISTRY

Growing small is also a prerequisite to effective personal ministry. How many prominent examples have we seen of public figures who have been disgraced because their largesse became the focus of their ministry? I believe that one of the greatest examples of growing small in ministry (that I have personally witnessed) is that of my late grandmother, Mrs. Minnie H. Penn. As a youth, I watched her serve other people through her gift of baking. And, bake she did—cakes, pies, cupcakes, turnovers, and much more. And she made clear to her grandson (me) and others who criticized her for not charging more money for her goods, that she did it "to make people happy." I did not fully appreciate it during her lifetime. But, I came to realize that my grandmother baked as her ministry. She was powerful, not because of her gift, but because of her humble posture. At her funeral, civil and religious dignitaries from around the country honored this "uneducated" woman for her lifetime of influence. Thousands were blessed (not to mention well-fed) by her smallness.

When your important relationships are strained, exasperation often leaves you questioning whether there is anything left in these relationships in which you can believe. But, there is real hope.

The hope, of course, lies in the greatest example of growing small that the world has ever known: Jesus Christ. God, the Father, in all His majesty sent His son Jesus down from glory to be born into this world as a human baby among the lowest rung

---

[94] Sanders, T., *Love Is the Killer App: How to Win Business and Influence Friends.* 2002: Crown Business, p. 12.

of Jewish society to redeem the sins of all humanity. Jesus modeled what it means to grow small. His posture is clearly evidenced in Matthew as Jesus said, "whoever would be great among you must be your servant, and whoever would be first among you must be your slave, even as the Son of Man came not to be served but to serve, and to give his life as a ransom for many" (20:26-28). And, it is only through our faith in Him and our servant-heartedness that we can discover greatness along our path to purpose.

While many of us lose sight of God when things are going well, our relational stumbles have a way of creating the sense of desperation that we most need to renew our connection with the Lord. And, just when you are tempted to succumb to your negative surroundings, remember the Lord's promise in 1 Corinthians 10:13, "God is faithful, and he will not let you be tempted beyond your ability, but with the temptation he will also provide the way of escape, that you may be able to endure it."

Mark's Gospel shows that our direction, fueled by the love for God and others, places us near the kingdom of heaven: "he [Jesus] said to him, 'You are not far from the Kingdom of God'" (12:34). But, Matthew (18:3) conveys that it is only through growing small, as modeled by Jesus, that the kingdom is truly attained. Direction and posture are complementary forces in building successful relationships. Your efforts to lovingly steward your relationships (direction) are enabled and sustained by your deliberate efforts to grow small (posture) through them.

Hopefully, your Spirit senses the biblical imperative to grow small. But, it may still feel like an elusive concept that is difficult to put into practice. The Apostle Paul learned through both choice and providence the necessity and power of growing small in achieving his purpose and in building winning relationships.

During our childhood, many of us used height charts, or maybe simple tick marks on our bedroom doorframe, to monitor how quickly we were growing up. Innately, most of us desire to measure how well we are progressing toward a desired goal. With this in mind, I would like you to consider the following ten signs to gauge your progression on your path to growing small. As you pass each milestone, take time to reflect on your journey and thank God for the relationships that He has placed along your path.

10 Signs that you are Growing Small

1. You are slowing down your reaction time to incendiary comments directed toward you.
2. It is getting easier for you to be excited for someone else who achieved a milestone that you are still working toward.
3. You can quickly apologize when you realize that you did something wrong and when others' feelings are hurt, even if it isn't clear that you did anything wrong.
4. Your ability to empathically listen to others is improving.
5. You have become more vulnerable in sharing your emotions and difficult life events with others.
6. You search for wisdom and seek to diligently practice what you discover.
7. You are increasingly more motivated by concern for the welfare of others, beyond what you can get out of the relationship.
8. Your self-awareness is heightened and you are comfortable being your authentic self in whatever space you occupy.
9. Your life's purpose and your unique voice have become clearer to you.
10. Your spiritual core affirms your physical and emotional decision-making.

CHAPTER 16:

ACCUMULATE GENEROSITY

"Give, and it will be given to you. Good measure, pressed down, shaken together, running over, will be put into your lap. For with the measure you use it will be measured back to you."

(LUKE 6:38)

The third and final aspect of loving wholeheartedly is about sharing yourself with others. To love wholeheartedly is to give generously. But, love is how you act, more than what you say. It reminds me of one of my favorite songs of my youth by the gospel group Commissioned, titled "Love Isn't Love," from their 1986 album Go and Tell Somebody. I love the lyrics from that song, but particularly the chorus: "Love isn't love/'til you've given it away/It's just waited to be given/all bitterness erased."[95] We have talked a lot about love. But, love is ultimately about generosity in giving. Of course, this is central to the gospel message. God gave His Son, Jesus Christ, to redeem mankind. Christ gave His life to cleanse our inequities. We give ourselves to connect others (and ourselves) back to Christ. This is the

---

[95] Commissioned, "Love Isn't Love," in Go Tell Somebody. 1986, Light Records.

circular nature of generosity. This is why scripture touts that "it is more blessed to give than to receive" (Acts 20:35). Giving makes a statement about trust. Giving is an act of faith that builds upon the premise that it is God, rather than ourselves or another human, who is the source of all that we have. Giving emerges from an abundance mindset.

We give when we trust that the reward that we get back is greater than the gift. To be clear, that reward is not always a physical item. Often, it is an emotional or psychological one. Emotionally, the reward may be experiencing the happiness of someone about whom you care or feeling satisfied that God is pleased with you. Of course, it could also be expectation of a more tangible reward. As an example, consider Proverbs 18:24: "A man who has friends must himself be friendly" (NKJV). There is a law of giving in effect here. Giving friendliness to others engenders friendliness towards you.

As important as it is to follow your passion and hone your voice, these efforts are powerless without a love for sharing or giving to others. Simply put, without sharing there is no influence. Sharing, in this context, takes on many forms. It is sharing your GODprint, resources, network, time, and even your faith. It is giving what you have to another. But, sharing happens most organically and altruistically when the issues of vulnerability and humility have been addressed. When you were a young child, your caregivers probably worked hard to instill the value of sharing with you. However, as we get older, sharing often loses its priority in our lives. We can talk endlessly about becoming love. But, you can never become love unless you first give it.

I like the way inspirational speaker Les Brown describes it as a universal law of giving and receiving in effect.[96] In Christian

---

[96] Brown, L., The Power of Giving. 2014 [cited 2015]; Available from: http://www.mindofsuccess.com/les-brown-quotes-power-of-giving/.

circles, it is often couched as the "principle of sowing and reaping." The idea is that what you invest in others is returned to you, particularly when given in love. Giving and receiving are not two separate concepts, as we tend to think; rather, they are two sides of the same continuum. Generosity is a grace. Here is one way to visualize it . . . When you open your hands to give, your hands are in the perfect position to receive. Conversely, when you live in a close-fisted way, you short circuit your ability to receive.

Though not usually taking the same form or from the same person, what you give out to the universe is returned to you. In the financial arena, the term "return on investment" (ROI) is used to depict the monetary gain resulting from an investment. Generosity's ROI, however, is gauged in a different unit of measure—relational equity. Relational equity is earned status or credits that you accrue based on the good rapport that you've established.

Your second shift influence is directly proportional to the relational equity that you accrue with your tribe. When you give generously of yourself, the trajectory of your influence grows exponentially—extending beyond the relational and into the spiritual realm.

OBEDIENT GENEROSITY

The Book of 1 Kings, chapter 17, provides an excellent model of the supernatural impact of being generous in your life through the experience of the prophet Elijah. Because of the wickedness of the king of Israel, the prophet Elijah pronounced that God would allow a drought to befall the country for more than three years. Though God supernaturally provided Elijah with food during the early period of the drought, God eventually instructed Elijah to journey to Zarephath for his continued sustenance. God told Elijah that in Zarephath (which means "a place of refining") he would meet a widow whom God had instructed to supply Elijah with food. Upon entering the city, Elijah spotted the widow and asked her to bring him some bread. The poor widow informed Elijah that she was simply gathering a few sticks of wood so that she could return home and use her little remaining flour and oil to make what she expected to be their final meal. But, Elijah tested her faith with an invitation to demonstrate her trust in God by using the last of her provisions to first serve Elijah a meal. Elijah informed her of God's promise of limitless flour and oil if she would be obedient to this instruction. The widow decided to obey God's instruction. Scripture informs us that, as promised, the widow, her son, and Elijah had food every day during the drought.

For much of my life, I have been familiar with this amazing story of Elijah and the widow. However, I have always interpreted it through the lens of obedience to God — which, of course, is a key component. Elijah demonstrated obedience to God in going to Zarephath without any idea of how he would actually meet this widow that God told him about. Even when Elijah encountered her, I can only imagine how he felt to learn that she had little food for him. Of course, there is also the obedience of the widow who was asked by a complete stranger to give him a portion of her and her son's meager last meal. We know that God had spoken to her already that Elijah was coming, but she still had to obey God and Elijah's solemn request. So, yes. This story is about obedience — more specifically, it is a story about obedient generosity.

> Your obedience to God unlocks doors
> for someone else.

Obedience to God unleashes His generosity towards His people. But, that isn't the end. What most astounds me is how godly obedience triggers generosity among people. In other words, your obedience to God unlocks doors for someone else. You become the conduit through which God's blessings flow to another. Of course, these blessings are providentially returned to you. Proverbs 11:25 captures it this way, "A generous person will prosper; whoever refreshes others will be refreshed" (NIV). Prosperity is generosity's fruit.

The story of God, Elijah, and the widow provides a model example of loving wholeheartedly through generosity. This story unveils the three tests of godly generosity. Godly generosity always tests your love in three domains: your fears (psychology), your faith (spirituality), and your fruit (productivity). Godly generosity challenges you to love by opening your mind to God moments without fearing the uncertainty that these moments evoke. Godly generosity admonishes you to love by obeying God's leading without regard to your own predilections. Finally, godly generosity measures the relational utility of what you produce. Let's look at each of these in more detail.

FEARLESS GENEROSITY

Elijah understood fear and vulnerability. He faced the threat of death on many occasions as Queen Jezebel sought to destroy him and other prophets of God. He and other prophets had hid themselves in caves to evade her capture. Fear was no stranger to Elijah. But, Elijah also understood godly generosity. After the widow's hopeless lament that she simply planned to fix their last meal and die, Elijah went right to the emotion that she was experiencing—fear. Fear for the life of her son and herself. Elijah immediately responded, "Do not fear; go and do as you have said. But first make me a little cake of it and bring it to me, and afterward make something for yourself and your son" (1 Kings 17:13). Elijah challenged the widow to take control of her emotions and obey generosity. What stands in the way of your generosity and mine? Fear. Why does loving wholeheartedly evoke such fear? It is because we are afraid of losing our own self-sufficiency. We are afraid that we will be taken advantage of by those we are trying to help. We are afraid that we will lose the modicum of control that we have left. We fear vulnerability. The DRAGONS magnify these fears to the point of paralysis. So, Elijah dealt immediately with the widow's DRAGONS in admonishing her to not have fear.

Let's not be unrealistic. Most of us will continually be challenged to face our fears. That is the nature of our humanity. For most of us, fear happens when faced with uncertainty or desperation. But, desperation has a way of simplifying the options. The widow's options seem clear when looking from the outside. Disobey God and die. Obey God and trust. Notice that I did not say her option was to obey God and live, because all she had were the words of Elijah. Would she trust that God would provide or would she choose to die? This is not just a story about trust between God, Elijah, and a widow. This story is about generosity in the face of fear. Loving wholeheartedly can only be done in the face of your fears, because it requires a level of generosity that pushes you to relinquish your perception of control and increase your trust in what you believe (not necessarily in what you see). Fearless generosity is the choice to obey God's command to give your life's sustenance to Him and trust that He will provide what you need. Many of us struggle to do that. But, as with the widow, when desperation arises, the choices become simple if you will yourself to objectively consider them. Disobey God and die with unfulfilled dreams, or obey God and trust that the universe will return your generosity to you.

FAITHFUL GENEROSITY

After dealing with the matter of fear, the second dimension of wholehearted generosity taps into the core of your belief system by asking you to consider where your faith lies. Faithful generosity suggests that your giving reflects what you believe to be true. In the story of Elijah and the widow, Elijah spoke to this woman's faith in God in saying, "For this is what the Lord, the God of Israel, says: 'The jar of flour will not be used up and the jug of oil will not run dry until the day the Lord sends rain on the land'" (1 Kings 17:14, NIV).

Why should she trust her last meal to a stranger? Why be generous when you are at the end of your own strength? She acted generously because she believed God's promise. In turn, her generosity to the Lord's servant was the catalyst for miraculous generosity bestowed upon her.

Sometimes, however, I think that we minimize the difficulty of faithfulness when we see it in the lives of others. Conversely, we tend to feel overwhelmed with this challenge when it applies to us. The widow initially responded to Elijah's request for food from the position of facts. It was true that she only had a little. It was true that she was just gathering sticks as a fire starter to prepare her last meal. It was true that she believed that she and her son were about to die. These were the facts.

> Faithful generosity is giving that prioritizes one's belief over apparent circumstance.

How often have the facts of the situation stunted your trust in God's provision? The problem, of course, is that we inherently see the facts of the matter as bigger than God. We wouldn't say that, of course, but our action reflects it. In most instances, we know that God could move on our behalf in the desperate situation. But, we just are not convinced that He will. Because we are not sure what God will do, we feel compelled to act on our own accord.

Faithful generosity is giving that prioritizes one's belief over apparent circumstance. In doing so, we affirm our conviction that God is bigger than the facts of the matter. The difficult circumstances around you may not immediately dissipate. As in the case of the widow, the drought remained a reality. However, faithful generosity provides for you in the midst of the trial. Whether you are on the mountain top or in the valley right now, the message is the same. Your demonstration of faith in God's promise will continually yield His blessings in your life— sometimes miraculously so. Faithful generosity doesn't give out of a desire to coerce God's positive regard towards us. It simply doesn't work that way. Rather, it expresses a posture of openness to divine provision towards us and through us.

FRUITFUL GENEROSITY

The final leg of the generosity triangle is fruitfulness. Godly generosity always produces relational fruit. Generosity matures your spiritual relationship with God and with other people. We have examined the importance of embracing vulnerability and humility as central elements of loving wholeheartedly. These are necessary prerequisites for spawning a generosity cycle that extends far beyond our own understanding.

During the early part of the drought, God supernaturally provided food and water to Elijah by using ravens and a brook. God could have continued this as a means of provision for Elijah for the entirety of the drought. So, why did God allow the brook to dry up? Why did God send Elijah to Zarephath to find a widow? I believe God was making a point about the fruit that emerges when generosity ensues. It is a matter of life and death.

As the story of Elijah and the widow unfolds, a dire crisis emerges. We learn that the widow's son became gravely ill and died. In her distress, the widow blamed Elijah. She was befuddled as to how this travesty could occur in the presence of God's man. Elijah neither hemmed nor hawed. Elijah's response was powerful. "Give me your son," he insisted.

When Elijah initially arrived, he solicited the widow's generosity in asking her to give him bread. Her generosity led to the miraculous supply of bread. But, it also released something even more powerful—a force that I call the "generosity snowball." The snowball represents the accumulation of generosity. It happens because, by nature, generosity releases reciprocity. Like the snowball that enlarges as it rolls through the snow, generosity balloons in scope and impact as it is paid forward. Elijah and the widow witnessed this generosity snowball firsthand. In the presence of ultimate despair, Elijah could say to the widow "give me your son." Elijah's pleas to God on the son's behalf brought him back to life. But, it all began with obedience to generosity. What a powerful display of generosity's fruitfulness.

GENEROSITY PHILOSOPHY

> Each of us will face that day when we need to breathe life into the death experience of another.

We never know the end result of our generosity. We just have to make that first decision to trust God's promise, even when the facts look grim. We do not have to revert to biblical days to witness marvelous demonstrations of the generosity snowball. Kim Trumbo, whom I introduced to you in an earlier chapter, lives this snowball effect every day through her organization, Generosity Philosophy. In her own words, Kim's mission is to share stories of generosity in order to inspire people to get involved out there in this huge world. Kim envisions a generosity movement.

Through her website, generosityphilosophy.com, and her Generosity Philosophy podcast, she pushes that generosity snowball for all our benefit.[97] Kim's is but one example of generosity's fruitfulness. I believe that each of us will face that day when we need to breathe life into the death experience of another. When that time comes, will you love wholeheartedly through generosity?

We see from the story of Elijah and the widow that the cycle of generosity begins and ends with God's intervention. God is the center of all wholehearted generosity. He is at the core of the snowball. Why? Because God uses generosity to build relationships which turn the hearts of people back towards him. Like Kim Trumbo posits, generosity is a philosophy. But, it is also theology. As with the whole nature of loving wholeheartedly, generosity points us back to the very nature of God. Generosity only makes sense in the context of others. We each have to ask ourselves, what is our generosity producing? But, the answer to that question always emerges from your obedience to God's directive to fearlessly and faithfully give your best to Him first.

THE LOVE SLAVE

We began this section on becoming love with the words of Jesus, who instructed His disciples that the greatest commandment is to love God and our neighbor. The question, however, was what that looks like in our daily lives. Over the past three chapters, I hope that you can see love as an energy of personal and relational transformation. Loving God and your neighbor can only be accomplished by loving yourself—who God made you to be. There is, in fact, no difference between loving God and loving yourself. They are inseparable. You cannot love your neighbor and not love yourself. They, too, are inseparable. What we are left with is the challenge to become the

---

[97] Trumbo, K. Available from: GenerosityPhilosophy.com.

love that God requires us to give. This is a countercultural message. But, I am convinced that this is the transformational love that spawns the zeal for you to influence the world. As in the story of Elijah and the widow, it starts and ends with God. But, in between is the trust in Him and in each other. That is what it means to love wholeheartedly with a posture of transparency and authenticity. The Apostle Paul coined one of the greatest phrases on love in 1 Corinthians 13:13, "So now faith, hope, and love abide, these three; but the greatest of these is love." In the end, it is as Paul intimates in the aforementioned 1 Corinthians 9:19 — we are created to be a love slave.

The winning attitude is that love trumps all. As you walk wholeheartedly in love's liberty, an amazing thing happens. People follow your voice — slowly at first. But, as your generosity continues, the snowball grows. Your territory enlarges. Your influence swells.

This influence comes with a responsibility to lead. As Luke 12:48 says, "to whom much was given, of him much shall be required." Next, we will conclude this book with a perspective on leadership with a different emphasis than conventional leadership models. Over the next several chapters, you will come to understand redemptive leadership and how to leverage your newfound personal power to embody this grace and transform culture.

PART 5:

THE SACRIFICE OF INFLUENCE

CHAPTER 17:

THE CASE FOR REDEMPTIVE LEADERSHIP

"Find your voice and inspire others to find theirs."

—STEPHEN COVEY

In this final section of the book, we focus on leadership more explicitly. I hope, however, it is clear by now that we have, in fact, been discussing leadership all along. Leadership cannot be examined in a vacuum. It only makes sense in the context of relationship. First, your relationship with your Creator. Then, your relationship with yourself. And, finally your relationship with others. Leadership always begins within you and then flows out for others.

The term "leadership" is freely tossed about in our social circles. But, what does it really mean? The term "leadership" is relatively new to the English language, only being used within the past two hundred years.[98] More than fifty years ago, noted leadership guru Walter Bennis suggested, "the concept of leadership eludes us or turns up in another form to taunt us again with its slipperiness and complexity. So, we have invented

---

[98] Stogdill, R. M., *Handbook of leadership: A survey of the literature.* 1974, New York: Free Press.

an endless proliferation of terms to deal with it . . . and still the concept is not sufficiently defined."[99] Stogdill states that, "there are almost as many different definitions of leadership as there are people who have tried to define it." Still today, amidst organizational debacles, political scandals, and lapses in moral judgment, we can conclude that leadership remains an elusive enigma.

Despite unprecedented access to best practices in leadership, most organizations today still suffer from one or more of four flaws: (1) lack of shared vision, (2) insulated and homogenous decision-makers, (3) policies and practices that are inflexible and lacking adaptability, and (4) lack of agility for the system to respond to new information.

Historically, leadership theorists have focused their models narrowly on either the personality traits, situational context, behavioral patterns, or functional outcomes of leaders. In recent years, however, more effort has been made to understand leadership as a dynamic integration of all of these facets. In my own dissertation research, I explored the applicability of one such integrated model called the Transformational Leadership Model, developed by Bernard Bass.[100] I was interested in this model because it sought to understand how to develop people who rise above the status quo to lead in extraordinary ways. The good news is that our understanding of leadership is evolving — though more slowly than most of us would like.

While a precise definition of leadership remains hard to pin down, leadership literature tends to agree on its three most basic components: group, influence, and goal. In other words, what we believe is that leadership entails intentionally guiding people toward a goal.

---

[99] Bennis, W. G., "The problem of authority." Administrative Science Quarterly, 1959: pp. 259-260.
[100] Bass, B. J. A. B. M., *The full-range of leadership development*. 1991, Binghamton, NY: Center for Leadership Studies.

Leadership is not about you. That is the big problem with leadership in our culture. Leaders believe that leadership is about their vision, their journey, and their dedication. That is not as it should be. If it is all about you, then walk your path alone. You don't need others, if it is your show. Leadership is intended to be about something transcendent. Leadership is really about those who follow.

> Redemptive leadership requires that you walk by faith, because that is the only way that you can see the possibilities that lie in those people who you lead.

Former GE CEO and motivational speaker Jack Welch says, "Before you are a leader, success is all about growing yourself. When you become a leader, success is all about growing others."[101] Leadership is cultivating the gifts, passions, and interests of the people that follow you—your tribe. As we have discussed, it is attentively listening to your tribe. It is authentically loving them with the best of who you are. And, only then, have you earned the right to lead them. The operative word here is "earned." Leadership is earned. It is instructive to examine that word "earn" more closely. The etymology of the word means to "do harvest work." I find that to be such powerful imagery. Leadership is harvesting. But, as any farmer will tell you, you can only harvest what you have sown and grown. If you didn't seed and grow it, you have to ask yourself if you have earned the right to harvest in that garden.

---

[101] Kruse, K., 100 Best Quotes on Leadership. 2012 [cited 2015]; Available from:
http://www.forbes.com/sites/kevinkruse/2012/10/16/quotes-on-leadership/.

HARVESTING EMOTIONAL COURAGE

There have been enough books written on leadership to fill its own library. Leadership development programs are a dime a dozen. With so much literature and so many programs available on the subject of leadership, why is it that actual leadership seems largely unsuccessful in most organizations?

Peter Bregman gives us a clue when he says that "the problem is the gap between what we know about leadership and what we do as leaders."[102] The question, of course, is why the gap exists when we have so much knowledge about leadership. I believe that the answer lies not in what we know cognitively — our knowledge base — we stumble because too little emphasis is placed on what we need to become as a result of that knowledge. Bregman argues that it is only through incorporating emotional courage into our leadership programs that they will ever become more effective. Leadership models applied in military to community contexts have certainly extolled the virtues of courage and engaging risk for the greater good of the team. That is nothing new. But, Bregman's assertion about emotional courage tackles the problem from a different angle — one's own emotional core.

Let's look closer at courage. The formal definition orients around the will of mind and spirit to face difficult circumstances without fear. I take some exception to that definition. I believe that courage is best understood when bravery is shown, even in the face of fear. Emotional courage then is the sheer force of will you exert to understand and direct your feelings in support of your goal-directed behavior — even in the face of extraordinary real and perceived risks. This, of course, is in contrast to what so

---

[102] Bregman, P., Why So Many Leadership Programs Ultimately Fail. 2013 [cited 2015]; Available from: https://hbr.org/2013/07/why-so-many-leadership-program.

commonly happens when your feelings dictate your decisions—which often lands you in a less than ideal place. This practically means that your emotions do not sabotage your dreams or hold them hostage. The reality of your emotions is accepted, but put in the broader context of your faith.

For much of this book, we have focused on who you need to become in your own pursuit of influence—particularly when pursued on the second shift. We examined how to embrace a KINGDOM attitude to tame those DRAGONS who would sap your emotional fortitude and courage. We considered how to follow the sound of your passions to discover those pivotal junctures demanding a courageous response. And, we have been challenged to embody the greatest emotion—love. Loving wholeheartedly is countercultural. But, it is without question the path to what Christ deemed the greatest commandment to love God and your neighbor.

Emotional courage is an amalgam of these interacting forces. That path is circuitous. But, it takes you to your dreams. Your GODprint will direct you to destiny's path. But, what will push you along that path when life presents difficult challenges? How will you generate enough willpower to stay focused on your vision as the DRAGONS vie for your attention? What will sustain your faith in God's providence in the face of risks that seem overwhelming? The answer to each of these questions is emotional courage. Fueled by wholeheartedness (authenticity and vulnerability), emotional courage pushes you along for the long haul. It strips you down of all pretense until your GODprint remains as the primary arbiter of your motivations. When your GODprint directs your steps, leadership and influence are inevitable byproducts. You were built for this.

This is precisely why leadership cannot be learned in a classroom. Rather, it is honed amidst life's complexities—chiseled through everyday battles, decisions, and risks. One can never say that he knows about flying a plane based on hundreds of hours in a training simulator. He only becomes a pilot from the mental and physical rigors of flying a real plane. Similarly, you only become a leader when you accept the risks and rewards of inspiring people towards a desired objective. This is why I appreciate Covey's assertion in his book, *The 8th Habit: From Effectiveness to Greatness*, that greatness only happens by finding your voice and using it to inspire others to do the same. By any definition, that satisfies the three elements of leadership—group, influence, and goal. Covey sees leadership "as a choice to deal with people in a way that will communicate to them their worth and potential so clearly they will come to see it in themselves."[103] US President John Quincy Adams captured the same idea about leadership in saying, "If your actions inspire others to dream more, learn more, do more and become more, you are a leader."[104]

But, you first have to dream, learn, do, and become more yourself before you can inspire others to do the same. No one of great influence circumvents this process. True leaders know that you can't grow where you won't go. Influential leaders exhibit the emotional courage to grow first. Personal growth then has a spillover effect, which positions them as redemptive leaders. Without compromising the primary objective, redemptive leaders exhibit ten practices that transform the world around them.

10 PRACTICES OF REDEMPTIVE LEADERS

Redemptive leaders...

---

[103] Covey, S., *The 8th Habit: From Effectiveness to Greatness*. 2013: Simon and Schuster.
[104] Luttrell, M., "John Quincy Adams perfectly defined leadership." 2011 [cited 2015]; Available from:
http://www.northbaybusinessjournal.com/csp/mediapool/sites/NBBJ/IndustryNews/story.csp?cid=4180440&sid=778&fid=181 - page=2.

1. Cast a vision that requires supernatural intervention
2. Sacrifice themselves to develop the possibilities that lie within the individuals they lead
3. Place people before policies
4. Prioritize integrity as an individual and corporate responsibility
5. Encourage failure because they know it is the precursor to growth
6. Apply grace liberally
7. Insist on personal stewardship
8. Reward strategic collaboration
9. Foster creative innovation
10. Resist one-size-fits-all solutions in favor of individualized consideration.

Regardless of whether you pursue your passion on the first or second shift, our world needs you to model redemptive leadership. This style of leadership requires the ability to listen and love your tribe with an open mind and heart, while staying true to your core identity. Redemptive leadership is having the vision for transformation, passion to inspire others to believe, and the dogged will to see it through.

> Brokenness is often the pivotal step to greatness.

Over the next several chapters, the key tenets of redemptive leadership are expounded upon as a guide along this journey of redemption. Why do we prioritize redemption? It is about brokenness. The journey to influence and leadership is rife with brokenness. We tend to think of brokenness with a negative connotation—sometimes deservedly so. However, brokenness is often the pivotal step to greatness. Redemption transforms brokenness. With redemption, a broken will supplants selfishness with selflessness. Redemption exchanges broken assumptions with faithful beliefs. Redemption replaces broken relationships with covenant partnerships. When we hear those stories of tests that became testimonies and messes that became messages, it is always about redemption.

Those of us in the Christian tradition understand that redemption is the bridge that connects us to God. Christ himself redeemed our sinfulness so that we can be presented as faultless before God. Redemption is a faith bridge that is supported by pillars of grace. Redemptive leaders stay connected to the divine source from which redemption, faith, and grace flow—allowing them to see situations and people, no matter how challenging, as hopeful and purposeful. In a world clamoring for sensitivity, stewardship, and integrity, there is no greater charge or case for redemptive leadership.

CHAPTER 18

SACRIFICE SECURITY

"Security is mostly a superstition. It does not exist in nature, nor do the children of men as a whole experience it. Avoiding danger is no safer in the long run than outright exposure. Life is either a daring adventure, or nothing."

– HELEN KELLER

Security is a primal need. The oldest part of our brain, the amygdala, is critical to human survival. It is responsible for detecting threats to our sense of security. The amygdala is a highly sensitive fear sensor. God designed us that way. The human ability to detect a threat and respond with an efficient "fight or flight" response was fundamental to human survival, particularly in the prehistoric era as dangers literally lurked around every corner. The number one daily goal was simply survival. In that setting, security was paramount.

Though most of us no longer need to worry about constant threats to our physical survival, that most basic part of our brain acts like we still do. Our brain works like an early detection system when it comes to real and perceived threats. In an effort to detect threats as early as possible, the brain's "elder statesman" works tirelessly to dissuade risk-taking behavior. To the amygdala, risk equals threat. Threat engenders fear. For the amygdala, fear means insecurity to which a "fight or flight" response is warranted. While other parts of the brain (such as the prefrontal cortex) are more risk tolerant, wired deep within your brain is a strong preference for security. For many, that inclination dissuades their conviction to be influential. Redemptive leaders push themselves and others through their primal emotion and sacrifice security because they know that growth and security are incompatible. You have to choose one and forsake the other. As with light and darkness, they cannot co-exist.

Security is an illusion.

Security is an illusion. Many of us struggle with this truism. Our culture tells us differently. Most of us have been socialized to believe that which is understood, quantified, and predictable is more secure. Conversely, ambiguity and unpredictability are risky and less secure. But, we have seen numerous instances in recent years where the established social convention proved flawed. We need only look at two colossal national collapses in the financial arena to see how security can be an illusion.

If you were fortunate enough to own information technology stocks in the late 1990s, you probably watched your portfolio soar. Encouraged by the bullish pundits, people were broadly encouraged to leverage as much as they could to invest speculatively in the next "can't miss" stock. Unfortunately, in 2001, billions of dollars in equity vanished as the US stock market plummeted in one of the biggest sell-offs in history. The pattern repeated in 2008 with the over-leveraged housing market. Pushed frenetically higher by unscrupulous lending practices, the mortgage business and housing prices were pushed to unprecedented levels in the early part of the twenty-first century. Conventional wisdom encouraged home purchasers to buy as much house as could be afforded. In their efforts to maximize profits, mortgage companies reduced the level of scrutiny on loan applications, with many even creating new loan products such as the zero-down loan, forty-year fixed-rate mortgages, and all sorts of adjustable rate mortgages to entice as many buyers as possible. Home prices were supposed to keep rising. There were few investments seen as more secure than a home purchase. But, in 2008 the housing bubble burst, with many homeowners trapped in mortgages that they could not afford and with little hope of selling homes with mortgages that exceeded their valuation. Security is an illusion.

The security illusion, however, is not confined to the financial markets. One of the most stark examples is in employment. Many of us have been socialized to equate predictably receiving a check every week or two from a stable employer as the model of security. That is certainly what I believed for much of my adult life.

As a young adult, my goal after receiving my undergraduate degree in Computer Information Systems was to work for IBM for thirty years and retire. With the dominant position that IBM held in the marketplace during the 1980s, that felt like a no-brainer from a security standpoint. While my departure from IBM after only five years of employment was unrelated to the decline in IBM's dominance, thousands of people lost their secure positions during IBM's drastic downsizing initiatives. This same scenario played out across many sectors as the national unemployment rate rose to levels that challenged our standing as a country. The days of expecting an employer to effectively guarantee you a secure, long-term position became extremely rare. Of course, with few exceptions, this security in employment has always been an illusion.

OUTSIDE THE COMFORT ZONE

Unfortunately, so many have also applied these flawed security assumptions to their own pursuit of influence. We tend to operate most of our lives in a comfort zone that does not trigger our amygdala's fear sensor. We avoid embarking upon too many risky endeavors so that we do not fail. We stick to the things and people that we know. We follow a "tried and true" routine that is familiar. And, we resist, sometimes forcefully, efforts to push us into the unfamiliar. The DRAGONS conspire to keep us at status quo.

> Obedience to God's call always leads you out of your comfort zone into the discomfort zone.

The reality, however, is that you can never pursue influence and stay in your comfort zone. Your growth only comes through your own personal quest to follow the sound of your passion. That sound inevitably leads you to God—the originator of your passion. Obedience to God's call always leads you out of your comfort zone into the discomfort zone. The discomfort zone stretches your belief about your life's purpose, the resources that you have, and what you feel you are capable of achieving.

Like Dorothy in The Wizard of Oz,[105] who followed the yellow brick road to the Emerald City, the discomfort zone is your path to destiny. You, like Dorothy, must adapt to life outside of Kansas. Kansas symbolizes that which is familiar. It is your comfort zone. Dorothy discovered much about herself and others by being forced by nature into unfamiliar and scary terrain, and encountering people with all sorts of issues. Given her displaced status, Dorothy took the advice of the Good Witch

---

[105] Fleming, V., The Wizard of Oz. 1939, Warner Bros.

Glinda, who informed her that maybe the much-heralded Wizard of Oz in the Emerald City could help her find her way back home. So, as instructed, she set her course to follow the yellow brick road to the Emerald City.

But, along her journey, Dorothy unexpectedly encountered three characters with deep-seated issues that are important to this discussion about security. Dorothy's first destiny partner was the Scarecrow. The Scarecrow sorrowfully lamented that only straw existed where his brain was supposed to be. He had not found his place in the world because he lacked the smarts or the intellectual capacity to find his way. As a result, the Scarecrow felt disempowered. His journey to the Emerald City was to claim the brains that would change the trajectory of his life—beyond being hung on a pole to ward off crows. The Scarecrow's desire represents the way that every pursuit of influence, by definition, entails a quest for knowledge and wisdom to know where to look for it. The knowledge that you have to succeed at your current level is not what you will need to master the next level. You will continually confront new challenges that require new approaches and insights. You cannot rest on your intellectual laurels. You must sacrifice the security in the knowledge that got you to where you are today, in order to make room for the intellect that you need for your next level of influence.

Dorothy's next encounter was with the Tin Man. The Tin Man was an emotional destitute. He had no heart. He lacked the capacity to feel and emotionally connect with the world around him. As such, he felt isolated and alone. The Tin Man's decision to partner with Dorothy reminds us to emotionally invest in others. Yes, relationships are risky and fraught with potential pitfalls. But, the reward is worth the risk because your purpose is always relational. Recognize, like the Tin Man, those areas where your emotional distancing is holding your destiny hostage. Invest emotionally in people that God places in your path. As you do this wisely, you sacrifice security by embracing the Tin's Man's Heart.

Finally, Dorothy encountered the Lion. Lions are supposed to be fierce and a model of bravery. Yet, this Lion was timid and lacked courage. As a result, the Lion felt shame. His decision to join Dorothy's pilgrimage informs us that every quest for purpose requires the courage to leave the familiar behind and align our reality with our destiny. You, too, must muster the Lion's courage to sacrifice security.

Your GODprint directs you to your own yellow brick road. Like Dorothy, the Lion, the Tin Man, and the Scarecrow, your own questions — and even your insecurities — are integral to your own quest. The DRAGONS want you to rest on your present successes. But, a KINGDOM mindset compels you to conjure the courage, emotional commitment, and intellect to risk sacrificing security.

When Dorothy and her three companions ultimately arrived in the Emerald City and finally gained an audience with the Wizard, they were quite dismayed to learn that the Wizard's "magical" abilities that they hoped to secure were an elaborate illusion. This is illustrative for your own journey. There is no silver bullet, no panacea. There is only the journey — the pursuit of influence. The journey to Oz was ultimately not about the Wizard's prowess. The journey was about who Dorothy, the Lion, the Tin Man, and the Scarecrow became through the journey. It was about whether they would cast their trust and security in the Wizard or in what was within them. When they sacrificed their security in the Wizard, they soon came to see that the journey had developed within them the very thing that their heart desired. The Lion demonstrated courage. The Tin Man proved his capacity to love. The Scarecrow showed he did indeed have brains. Dorothy, of course, proved herself to be a redemptive leader of this motley crew. With this experience, she was ready to return home as a new person.

Your pursuit of influence is no different. You, too, must muster the Lion's courage, the Tin Man's heart, and the Scarecrow's intellect to navigate through uncomfortable situations and decisions. As a redemptive leader, you must also cultivate the courage, emotionality, and cognition in others—even in the face of their resistance.

> The truth is that "security" can only be found in what the Creator of the universe is doing within you.

The primary point of this chapter is that so many of our human institutions are built on assumptions that tend to shift over time. Ultimately, our deep search for meaning and security cannot be found in such institutions or any other external entities, because they are outside of your control. The truth is that "security" can only be found in what the Creator of the universe is doing within you. But, you will only discover this when you leave Kansas—your comfort zone. Your destiny is in your discomfort zone, because that is where your destiny demands more of you.

You, like Dorothy, are sure to face the Wicked Witches and flying monkeys that seek to derail or even destroy you. But, the more time that you spend in your discomfort zone, the quicker you will acclimate to its challenges. Your discomfort will eventually become more comfortable, and the cycle begins yet again. I call this the Cycle of Sacrifice—moving from comfort to discomfort to comfort. That is the path of the redemptive leader. You must find your security in its rhythm.

CHAPTER 19

FAIL FORWARD

"Life is playing a poor hand well. The greatest battle you wage against failure occurs on the inside, not the outside."

– JOHN MAXWELL

The second shift is an amazingly rewarding journey. But, let's face it. It is also a difficult road. Time feels compressed. Resources feel stretched. Progress feels slow. It's about feelings. But, your feelings are not reliable markers of your leadership potential. Feelings are temporal. They sway with the wind of time. If you base your leadership beliefs on your feelings, you will inevitably lose sight of your core WHY, as Simon Sinek encourages.[106]

Rather than feelings, think of leadership as being about faith—a belief that you are moving in a direction that warrants the attention of others. Faith, not feelings, is the best barometer of your potential to lead redemptively. Redemptive leadership requires that you believe through faith what you cannot yet see. Redemptive leadership requires faith in God, in people, and in

---

[106] Sinek, S., *Start with Why: How Great Leaders Inspire Everyone to Take Action*. 2009: Portfolio.

yourself. Redemptive leadership requires faith in the process and the potential of listening and loving well.

> You can never be a redemptive leader without faith, because what you literally see will always confound you.

In the early days of developing your second-shift influence, you will feel as if you are alone. Few, if any, people are reading the content that you spent hours developing. No one leaves comments on your blog posts. Though you know that you are supposed to grow your email list, the new subscribers are few and far between. The groups that you have paid to join do not seem to give you the return on the investment that you expected. You feel like you are expending a lot of effort—juggling so many balls. You wonder if you have what it takes to do this for the long term. It seems so easy for others. Here is a truism: If your decision to continue your pursuit of influence is based on what you see and feel, you will not succeed.

Even after your second-shift influence begins to get some traction, the challenge of faith continues. When you have experienced some success, the temptation is to again start believing what you see. If you are not careful, you will give too much credit to your efforts, strategic partners, or maybe blind luck. Yes, these contribute to your success. But, it is your faith more than anything else that pushes the trajectory of your influence.

FAIL YOUR WAY TO SUCCESS

> Failure is not a wasted effort. Failure is a learning experience. Failure is the new success.

I have come to believe something that sounds remarkably unbelievable on its face: Failure is the new success. As more people explore their entrepreneurial chops, it is fascinating to hear the litany of thought leaders exploring the importance of failure. Rather than seeing failure as something to be avoided, they say to embrace it. Success is only achieved through trial and error that is, by definition, rife with many failures. Pundits admonish nascent entrepreneurs to not let their fear of failure stymie their purposeful pursuits. They encourage you to push through your failures, one after another, until you find your dream. The idea, of course, is that failure is not a wasted effort. Failure is a learning experience.

All failure, however, is not created equal. If you allow failure to become your albatross, that is not helpful. If repeated failure somehow poisons your psyche or diminishes your convictions, that is not helpful. I submit then the key is not just in the failing. Rather, it is important that you fail forward. What does it mean to fail forward? It is failure that advances your position in relation to your goal or objective. If from your failure you learned something that you did not know, that failure was a success. If from your failure you ruled out one possible option, then you have successfully improved your chances of success on the next test. Though most of us do not relish the thought of failing, if we are able to fail forward we know that we are better off than when we started. You are making progress towards your objective.

Redemptive leaders are successful because they reframe what is experienced as a negative failure into a positive experience of failing forward. In his first inaugural address on March 4th, 1933, in the midst of the Great Depression, US President Franklin D. Roosevelt coined the famous quote, "The only thing we have to fear is . . . fear itself—nameless, unreasoning, unjustified terror which paralyzes needed efforts to convert retreat into advance."[107] Powerful words at a time of national crisis—reminding us that fear is often our worst enemy in our efforts to reach our goals. President Roosevelt understood that the biggest detractor to failing forward is fear. Fear pushes our failure in the wrong direction. One of the most prevalent fears is a fear of failure. While everyone has some trepidation about something, according to Psychology Today this fear of failure is so great that it overwhelms their motivation to succeed—often sabotaging their own chances of success and passionate pursuits.[108] But, I would like to propose a paradigm shift—one in which failure is welcome, and maybe even celebrated as the surest path to success. We all fail. That is a fact of life.

- Hall of fame baseball player, Ted Williams, is regarded as one of the greatest hitters in baseball history. But, he failed to get a hit nearly two-thirds of the time.
- In 1995, author J. K. Rowling completed her first Harry Potter novel, only to have it rejected by all 12 publishing houses to which it was sent.
- American inventor, Thomas Edison, is known for the litany of failures that he experienced on his journey to discovering the optimal filament for the light bulb.

Yes. Failure is real. But, success can be on the other side of failure—if you keep going and apply what you've learned along the way. If you fail forward, you succeed. The problem is when you stop—when you sulk, wallow, and commiserate with others

---

[107] Rosenman, S., ed. Franklin D. Roosevelt, Inaugural Address, March 4, 1933. The Public Papers of Franklin D. Roosevelt. Vol. Two: The Year of Crisis. 1938, Random House: New York.
[108] Winch, G. "10 Signs that you might have fear of failure...and 2 ways to overcome it and succeed." 2013[cited 2015]; Available from: https://www.psychologytoday.com/blog/the-squeaky-wheel/201306/10-signs-you-might-have-fear-failure.

who feel like a failure. You throw a pity party. The DRAGONS smile.

But, when you fail forward, you simply see it as putting you one step closer to your goal. There is no better example of this mindset than Thomas Edison. Edison's efforts assure us that success is not about being the smartest, the prettiest, or the luckiest. Rather, success is a commitment to consistency and persistency. And, you must be successful in your thinking before you can be successful in your doing. Successful thinkers understand that, as achievers, they must fail their way to success.

TEN STEPS TO FAIL FORWARD

I would like to propose ten steps that can shift your mindset about failure—allowing you to experience that paragon of success in your own life. For each step, I introduce an Edison quote to give evidence that failure is indeed the best path to success.

Step 1: Check your pride at the door.

"Discontent is the first necessity of progress."[109]
—Thomas Edison

Transforming failure to success requires that you not be so arrogant as to believe that errors and shortcomings are beneath you. By checking your pride at the door, you remove the proverbial blinders and permit yourself to accept (and maybe even laugh) when experience falls short of the goal. The humility that emerges from growing small allows us to learn from others and continually ask how we can do things better.

---

[109] Edison, T., *Diary and Sundry Observations of Thomas Alva Edison*, ed. D.D. Runes. 1948: Greenwood Pub Group.

Step 2: Expect and embrace failure as the cost of success.

"Many of life's failures are people who did not realize how close they were to success when they gave up."[110]
—Thomas Edison

When you allow yourself to see failure as a necessary step to great things, it becomes more acceptable and normalized. It doesn't catch you by surprise. I'm reminded of the times that I taught my children to roller-skate. I told them, "if you can't accept falling, you'll never be a good skater." Every time you learn something new on wheels, it is going to take a lot of falls to get there. Life goals are the same way. I like to think of it this way. If you're too afraid to fail, then you're too comfortable to succeed. Success requires desperation.

Step 3: Believe your idea is great until you're convinced it isn't.

"If we did all the things we are capable of, we would literally astound ourselves."[111]
—Thomas Edison

If you don't believe in your ideas, it is pretty unlikely that anyone else will, either. When you believe in something, it stirs your emotions. There is discontent and unrest until you see it come to fruition. It fuels your drive. There is an old adage that the richest land on earth is the graveyard, because so many people die with great ideas inside them. So, push your ideas.

If you're like me, some of your ideas won't stand the test of time. Some will need major adjustment. Others need to be discarded. That's fine. This is part of the refinement process.

---

[110] Headstrong, D., *From Telegraph to Light Bulb with Thomas Edison.* 2007: B&H Publications.
[111] Ford, M. E., *Motivating Humans: Goals, Emotions, and Personal Agency Beliefs.* 1992: Sage Publications.

Step 4: Consult with wise friends who are willing to hurt your feelings.

"We don't know a millionth of one percent about anything."[112]
—Thomas Edison

The insecure person is unwilling to have his ego bruised by constructive criticism. This person prefers someone to sing his praises and get a pat on the back rather than a true "iron sharpens iron" experience.

However, wisdom is evident when you stress test your ideas with people who can objectively scrutinize it. The wise person realizes his own limitations and continually seeks to improve himself and his ideas. High achievers surround themselves with others similar to—or smarter than—them to grow, while low and moderate achievers surround themselves with those less smart than them so they don't feel threatened. Growth comes when you "run with a pack" of those who love you enough to not just tell you what you want to hear and, as a result, push you beyond what you thought possible.

Step 5: Don't accept YES for an answer.

"To have a great idea, have a lot of them."[113]
—Thomas Edison

For the achiever, it feels good to hear the approval for your efforts. It's easy, however, for such approval to lull you into a false sense of security. Just because there are those who like your

---

[112] Stevenson, B. E., *Stevenson's Book of Quotations*. 3rd ed. 1931: Cassell & Company.
[113] Edison, T.; Available from: http://quotationsbook.com/quote/20072/.

idea, doesn't mean it is as good as it can be. The person who can't learn from failure subjects themselves to what psychologists call confirmation bias. In other words, you look for others to tell you what you want to hear.

You know the level of creativity inside you. Trust your gut. If you feel that your idea needs to be better, don't settle for others telling you it's good enough. Make it better. Or, at least, get more experienced eyes to assess its merit before deciding that it is as good as it gets. Sometimes, if it ain't broke, you need to break it and make it better.

Step 6: See every rejection as a step closer to the goal.

> *"Our greatest weakness lies in giving up. The most certain way to succeed is always to try just one more time."*[114]

—Thomas Edison

Ted Williams, J. K. Rowling, and Thomas Edison have proven the point. True greatness does not come without colossal failures. Why? Because these stumbles build the character that is necessary to be great. Failures build the persistence necessary for greatness. Knockdowns build that emotional courage to get back up. For the true achiever, tough situations strengthen your resolve. And, resolve is just a step away from greater success.

Step 7: Redefine success.

> *"Just because something doesn't do what you planned it to do doesn't mean it's useless."*[115]

—Thomas Edison

---

[114] Ibid.
[115] Ibid.

We are socialized to see success as a destination. We are successful when we make a million dollars or own our own business or have 10,000 followers on Twitter. Of course, this means that—up until that destination is reached—you were unsuccessful (or maybe even a failure). It's time for us to redefine success from a destination to a process. Success is becoming more caring, more determined, and more courageous (to name a few). So, the next time things don't work as planned, look for the lesson there that positions you to be a better person.

The story of 3M's Post-it Notes are a great example of redefined success. In 1968, Dr. Spencer Silver was attempting to develop a super-strong adhesive. But, his efforts kept falling short. They just were not sticky enough. Instead, he created what have become known today as Post-it Notes. Initially, his new invention was not well received—even within 3M. However, years later, a colleague, Art Fry, envisioned a practical use for it. And, twelve years after its original invention, Post-it Notes were launched in the US, Canada, and Europe to wide success. Sometimes, success just has to be redefined.

Step 8: Leverage the empathy to serve others at their moments of failure.

> "I have not failed. I've just found 10,000 ways
> that won't work."[116]
> **—Thomas Edison**

One of the most impactful aspects of experiencing failure is the empathy that it fosters for others with similar experience. You understand that feeling. You identify with the pain, angst, and frustration. That sense of identification can be a strong

---

[116] Edison, T., *Diary and Sundry Observations of Thomas Alva Edison*, ed. D. D. Runes. 1948: Greenwood Pub Group.

magnet, allowing you to wield significant influence with others. The adage is true. People want to know how much you care before they care how much you know. When you identify with their failings and help them see a better path, you touch a deep place in the heart of another.

Step 9: Share your failures to increase transparency and authenticity.

"Show me a thoroughly satisfied man and I will
show you a failure."[117]
—Thomas Edison

In a culture replete with pretense and fake celebrity, authenticity is golden. Sharing your own failures helps people relate to you. For many people, it normalizes their struggle. It fosters trust. When people trust you, they follow your lead. They buy your products. They recommend your brand. Rather than assuming that admitting failure will doom you, you are more likely to find that it will strengthen your relationships. It makes you relatable.

Step 10: Once you've reached a goal, push it until you fail again.

"There's a way to do it better. Find it."[118]
—Thomas Edison

When you reach a certain level of success, the stakes and risks often get higher. But, you've developed the character, skills,

[117] Edison, T.; Available from:
http://quotationsbook.com/quote/20072/.
[118] Finn, C.A., *Artifacts: An Archaeologist's Year in Silicon Valley.* 2002: The MIT Press.

and relationships to sustain that success. It can be easy at that point to rest on one's laurels. But, the great ones see possibilities beyond current success. They live with a continuous curiosity as to what can be done better. So, they push themselves out of the known and into less safe domains. They do so with wisdom and discernment. These people see something that others don't, and they won't be satisfied until they stretch for it.

I hope that you see how it is indeed possible (and usually even required) to fail your way to success. It's a reconceptualization that is rooted in an eternal optimism that you are created with purpose and wonder beyond what you can even imagine. For you, failure is an option. But, only when you fail forward. You have what it takes to be fail-proof and to lead others to be the same. Redemptive leaders fail forward.

CHAPTER 20

TAME TIME

"Lost time is never found again."

– BENJAMIN FRANKLIN

Last week, you were given precisely 168 hours to pursue your dream. If you're fortunate, this week will be the same. As long as blood courses through your veins each week, that same pattern will repeat—168. You see, time is constant. It is your most precious commodity because every second that passes is one that is lost forever. You will make more money. You will meet more people. But, you will never gain more time. Each week, it will always be 168 hours. Time is the great normalizer. It does not discriminate by ethnicity, gender, or social status. Benjamin Franklin said, "lost time is never found again."[119] You see, it is never a question of how much time you have—it is the same for everyone. The question, then, is whether last week's 168 took you closer towards your destiny.

For most of us, the 168 is comprised of family, work, school, church, and personal time. We are creatures of habit. So, for

---

[119] Bacharach, S., Stop Procrastinating: 5 Tips from Ben Franklin. Available from: http://www.inc.com/samuel-bacharach/stop-procrastinating-five-tips-from-ben-franklin.html.

most of us, last week's 168 will probably be very similar to this week's 168. So, when it comes to your role in the creation nation, odds are that if you made little progress last week, neither this week nor next are likely to be much different. I like William Penn's saying that "time is what we want most, but what we use worst."[120] Without a doubt, there is no greater determinant of your pursuit of influence than the manner in which you use the time that you are given. This is especially crucial for those of us on the second shift, because discretionary time is in such short supply. It is your most precious commodity to manifest your creative potential.

> Time is like a wild stallion that must be tamed to work towards your goals.

If you cannot harness time, your purposeful pursuit will be mercilessly thrown to the ground—metaphorically speaking. In recent years, I have learned something about myself. I fear time. For some people, that fear manifests as mid-life crisis that is experienced when disappointment exists around one's accomplishments. Other people fear time's monotony because their days are filled with hurts and anxiety.

For me, time is like a jar full of marbles. I specifically think of each marble as an hour. There is a finite number of marbles in the jar. Every single day, twenty-four of those marbles empty from my jar. How many are left? I don't know. But, I fear that one day, when my last twenty-four marbles sit in the jar, I may not have lived my life to its fullest potential. I want to feel in my last days that I have indeed maxed out my life. I want to feel that I gave it my all. As the sports lingo goes, I want to "leave it all on

---

[120] Penn, W., *Some fruits of Solitude in reflections & Maxims*. 2015: Leopold Classic Library.

the field." When that last marble drops out and my jar is empty, I want to feel like I gave everything that I have.

But, there is a fear. I fear that this stallion, with its spirited nature and unpredictable twists, will throw me from its unsaddled back and leave me lying broken on the ground. Rather than riding it to glory, I fear being another statistic—someone who had a lot of potential but never quite reached that tipping point to greatness. Yes, I can admit that I desire greatness. Is that selfish to say? Maybe, in some ways. But, I prefer to think of it in light of the previously cited admonition by the Apostle Luke: "Everyone to whom much was given, of him much will be required, and from him to whom they entrusted much, they will demand the more" (Luke 12:48).

Pursing full-time influence requires mastery of the margins of your life. Like an experienced bronco-busting cowboy, you must tame time to be a successful second-shift influencer. Taming time entails three components that help you to put it all in perspective and to carve out the necessary time for your passionate pursuits. First, you must remember that your calling is God's challenge—not yours. So, when faced with its demands, take it "easy and light" because you know that he is in control. Second, keep in mind that God's timing is usually not yours and mine. We must be patient and defer to God's timing rather than getting ahead of ourselves and acting prematurely. Finally, you simply have to commit the time on a daily basis to create according to your ability. Incremental effort to concentrate on the sound of your passion will yield extraordinary results over the long term. As you master these three components, time will feel like an ally rather than an adversary.

TAKE IT EASY AND LIGHT

I think of all the benefits that God has provided me. No, my life has not been that proverbial bed of roses. But, in so many ways I am tremendously blessed beyond measure. With this blessing comes a responsibility. That responsibility is to be great because I serve a God who is great. As I reflect and co-create with Him, I expect to be great. Greatness, however, is a gift that comes with responsibility to point other people to God and their own journey with Him. And, oftentimes the weight of that responsibility feels heavy—especially as I watch those marbles drop from my jar every day. I know in my head that God says that His yoke is easy and His burdens are light (Matthew 11:30). But, when I am most honest, I can admit that often I feel neither.

This instruction in the Book of Matthew is important because it makes three things clear as it pertains to time. First, God does place a "yoke" on us. The word "yoke" is typically used in the farming context to refer to a wooden beam that is placed on animals, usually oxen, to guide them to work together on a task. God places a yoke on you and me because we have a task set before us. So when God places a yoke on you, with whom is He pairing you? I submit that God's intention is that you are yoked to Christ. This divine pairing is a reference to Christ's redemptive work for you in dying on the cross—making eternal salvation available. But, it also refers to the co-creation process. When you partner with Christ, your creative potential is maximized because it reflects the synergy of you working with Him. God's yoke is divine and offers a perspective on time as both salvation- and purpose-oriented.

The second point about the Matthew 11 passage is the acknowledgement that God does indeed give us a burden. The word "burden" usually has a negative connotation for us. We think of it as implying something weighty that may be too much for us. But, the term simply suggests a task. So, as we think about time, we have to consider the tasks that God sets before us to accomplish within the time that is gifted to each of us.

The third point about this passage is that it is of utmost importance. It's God's promise to keep it "easy and light." God desires that we experience Him, not as a heavy weight, but as a burden that is "easy and light." Yes, God holds us accountable for the work, but that is the way our theology is framed. God asks us to cast our cares upon Him. Psalm 55:22 offers this encouragement: "Cast your cares on the LORD and he will sustain you; he will never let the righteous be shaken" (NIV). When we spend our time on-task and co-creating with Christ, we should be unshaken. How is that possible? It is an act of working with excellence on the tasks (the input), but releasing rather than worrying about the outcomes (the output).

When you fret incessantly about the results of your efforts, you can be easily discouraged. For some, that discouragement results in us sacrificing other important aspects of life—such as relationships and health—in order to put in more effort. For others, this discouragement leaves them sulking with a sense of defeat. Neither of these reactions are God-inspired. God intends that we put in our best effort but then release the output to Him. Our challenge is to trust Him with the output when we have done our best. The reality is that we cannot control the output, anyway. We can simply pray for God's will to be done. I do not mean to suggest that this release is easy because, for me, it is a constant source of tension. But, such a stance is the key to spending our time on purpose-driven work that is easy and light.

GET IN THE ZONE

I travel quite a bit in the United States, and sometimes abroad. In my day job (my first shift), I also work with people around the globe. One of the keys to success in my job is remembering the time zone of all parties involved in the exchange. I currently reside in the Eastern United States. But, when I travel abroad, I set my watch to the local time to make sure I am on time for my appointments.

When it comes to your pursuit of influence, you also have to understand that there are two time zones — Physical Time (PT) and Spiritual Time (ST). These two time zones operate on entirely different principles and assumptions. Physical time is chronological. Physical time looks at the years, months, days, and hours that that you can plan and measure using your calendar. For example, when we think about the 168 hours available each week, we are talking about physical time. As implied by its name, we know that there are certain realities in physical time as it is bound by time and space. The laws of physics apply.

Spiritual time, however, is not bound by physics or our Gregorian calendars. Instead, spiritual time is measured by purposeful growth and readiness. We get a glimpse of spiritual time in 2 Peter: "But do not overlook this one fact, beloved, that with the Lord one day is as a thousand years, and a thousand years as one day. The Lord is not slow to fulfill his promise as some count slowness, but is patient toward you, not wishing that any should perish, but that all should reach repentance" (3:8–9). This passage instructs us that God is not constrained to physical time. Rather, His objective focuses solely on your spiritual readiness. Not surprisingly, that usually does not comport with our own preferred timing.

> We can only tame time by understanding that God's plans for each of us are primarily oriented in spiritual, rather than physical time.

While physical time is about your progress towards time-limited goals, spiritual time is about your spiritual maturation and that of those to whom your GODprint directs you. We can only tame time by understanding that God's plans for each of us are primarily oriented in spiritual, rather than physical time. We,

241

therefore, have to trust in His spiritual timing because, as the scripture notes, "For as the heavens are higher than the earth, so are my ways higher than your ways and my thoughts than your thoughts" (Isaiah 55:9). God sees the big picture. He orchestrates spiritual time to maximize your spiritual growth and to position you for maximum impact on the growth of your tribe. Sometimes, God's plans fall within our physical time preferences. But, they usually do not. This is because God wants to develop your faith and trust in Him, and not in your own strength. In order to tame time, you must work in physical time with a spirit of excellence, while deferring to spiritual time for the outcome that is best for you.

DEFINE YOUR "WISH WINDOW"

> The "wish window" is that coveted time that you have each day to build your passion portfolio.

The third and final element of taming time is your schedule. Though spiritual time is the dimension in which God develops your spiritual identity, you can only maximize your second-shift influence by mastering your time margin. The only way to do this is to develop a sustainable plan. This section of the book outlines a simple and tactical plan to elevate your influence, regardless of the current size of your platform.

In 2013, the Bureau of Labor Statistics conducted an American Time Use Survey.[121] Though they reflect the average American and your situation might be different, the results reveal the secret to achieving extraordinary influence. Let's take

---

[121] American Time Use Survey. 2013 [cited 2015]; Available from: http://www.bls.gov/tus/.

a closer look at the results of the study. Not surprisingly, the largest time allocation for the weekday in America is work—averaging nearly nine hours. After work, sleeping is most time-consuming, at an average of eight hours. In other words, work and sleep alone account for seventeen hours—more than 70% of our 24-hour day. Household activities, eating and drinking, caring for others, and other activities account for another five hours. That leaves approximately two hours. So, what do we Americans do with those two hours? Leisure and sport.

First, let's keep it real. Everyone needs leisure. Leisure is important for rejuvenating our physical, psychological, and spiritual self. It should not be completely sacrificed for productivity. Each day, we must reserve some time for relaxation. But, what would be possible if you cut that leisure and sport time in half—down to one hour? The problem is that most people fail to leverage any of their discretionary time for passionate pursuits. But, just taking one hour each day to develop your presence on the second shift is all it takes to tame time and build greater impact. That one hour each day is what I call your "wish window," because it is what separates successful second-shift influencers from everyone else. The "wish window" is that coveted time that you have each day to build your passion portfolio and influence.

Many would-be influencers remain on the sidelines because they do not see how to fit their passion into their lives. They feel trapped with too little time and too big a dream. They literally do not believe they have enough time to do what they are called to do. But, it is a lie. It's the DRAGONS' deceit. If this describes you, let me assure you that you only need one hour—plus discipline. What you wish your passion to become can be achieved by how you manage your 1-hour "wish window"—that discretionary time block that you have every single day. In his book, *The 15 Invaluable Laws of Growth: Live Them and Reach Your Potential*, leadership expert John C. Maxwell said, "You will never change your life until you change something you do daily. The secret of your success is found in your daily routine."[122] Your one-hour wish window is the secret to your success.

Over a week, that one hour becomes seven hours — similar to a conventional work shift. This is your second shift. Over a month, it becomes 31 hours in your wish window. And, over a year, your diligence carves out 365 hours. Even if you take five days off for vacation, you still have 360 second-shift hours to listen, love, and lead your tribe. But, it all starts with one hour a day.

The question then becomes, what do you do to maximize that one hour? In his book, *The One Thing: The Surprisingly Simple Truth Behind Extraordinary Results*, Gary Keller posits that we should spend that one hour a day with the following focusing question, "What is the ONE thing that you can do this hour such that by doing it everything will be easier or unnecessary?"[123] Your ONE thing should be the focus of your wish window. Take some time to think about what that one thing might be for your wish window over the next seven days. For more specific suggestions about how to maximize your productivity in the wish window, I recommend Jonathan Milligan's excellent book, *The 15 Success Traits of Pro Bloggers*.[124] Whether or not you are (or aspire to be) a blogger, this book offers an excellent model and tactical tips for building an influential presence.

Your one thing may be developing and packaging inspirational content (e.g., videos, blog posts, articles) related to your passion, building relationships with other influencers and

[122] Maxwell, J., *The 15 Invaluable Laws of Growth: Live Them and Reach Your Potential*. 2014: Center Street.
[123] Keller, J. & Papasan, J., *The One Thing: The Surprisingly Simple Truth Behind Extraordinary Results*. 2013: Bard Press.
[124] Milligan, J., *The 15 Success Traits of Pro Bloggers: A Proven Roadmap to Becoming a Full-Time Blogger*. 2015: CreateSpace Independent Publishing Platform.

your tribe, or expanding your email distribution list. But, your one thing may also be introspective, prayerful, and listening to what God is speaking. The important thing to remember is to tackle a task and work it through to completion.

Every week, you will have 168 hours at your disposal. For those of us on the second shift, most of those hours are accounted for with first-shift responsibilities, sleeping, and sundry household duties. But, it only takes one hour a day in the physical time zone where you consistently focus on your ONE thing, while remaining confident that God will raise the harvest in His spiritual time. This is the proven formula for taming that wild stallion, while keeping it easy and light as God intends. As you do so, you model redemptive leadership in a culture that—to its detriment—consistently prioritizes temporal achievements over ones with eternal significance. They need you to lead them home.

CHAPTER 21

PROMOTE PARTNERSHIP

"Helped are those who create anything at all, for they shall relive the thrill of their own conception and realize a partnership in the creation of the Universe that keeps them responsible and cheerful."

– ALICE WALKER

The final step on the journey to becoming a redemptive leader is partnership. It is only fitting that this road to listen, love, and lead must end with a focus on relationship. You started down this road by following the sound of your passion. This path has led you to courageously face the DRAGONS, to embrace your place in the creation nation, and to listen, love, and lead as your GODprint inspires. This path is rewarding beyond measure. But, it is long and not for the faint of heart. It is an emotional roller coaster. There are periods of profound jubilation and moments of deep despair. This is all a necessary part of the growth experience. It is for this reason that, without exception, every person of extraordinary influence has one or more partners who accompany them for some or all of the journey.

From the beginning of mankind, God promoted many forms of partnership. According to the Book of Genesis, God gave Eve to Adam because God saw that it would be better if Adam were not alone. The Lord allowed Aaron to be a spokesman for Moses before Pharaoh in the Book of Exodus when Moses' self-confidence waned. The Book of 1 Samuel records David's reliance on Jonathan's brotherly love and wisdom to guide him through some difficult situations. There are many such examples. But, I believe that some of the most powerful demonstrations of partnership are evident with the Apostle Paul as he traversed through Gentile nations, preaching the gospel of Christ.

Paul is the front man and deservedly gets most of the credit for the spread of Christianity outside of the Jewish community in the early Church. There is, however, considerable evidence that the scope of his influence is rooted in the partnerships that God orchestrated. Paul's first partnership was with Barnabas, whose very name means "son of encouragement." Barnabas took the risk to vouch for Paul, even when other Christians still distrusted him because of his former life as a persecutor of the Church. But, inspired by the Lord, Barnabas helped introduce Paul to key church figures and help him acclimate to his new life in Christ—first in the city of Antioch and then beyond. Barnabas' penchant for encouragement is clearly evident. But, the partnership of Paul and Barnabas extended far beyond words and introductions. In fact, Barnabas believed so much in Paul's ministry that he actually put aside his own ministry to accompany Paul on a harrowing missionary journey that led to the establishment of churches in many cities, though not without physical torture and imprisonment.

The key point here is that, from the earliest points in human history until today, with few exceptions, partnership continues to be the cornerstone of great achievement. It is the key to your second-shift influence as well. Every influencer needs a Barnabas in his corner who speaks on his behalf, covers his back, and walks alongside him in pursuit of his influence. If you have not yet identified who that person is for you, be prayerful and watchful. If you have a sense of who your Barnabas is, treat him or her with the utmost respect, value, and trustworthiness.

Redemptive leadership, however, also treats partnership as more than a relationship that benefits your specific agenda. It is equally important to identify relationships into which you are called to invest time, wisdom, and resources. The term "mentor" is commonly used to characterize these types of relationships in which leaders intentionally cultivate the potential, interests, and gifts of others.

Effective partnerships can take many forms. But, modern history with its technological advantages seems to demonstrate ways in which groups, individuals, and even businesses can be effective partners for you. The format of the partnership may be less important than the idea of sharing one's vision with trusting others who can help you bring it to reality as efficiently as possible. As we examine the importance of partnership in expanding your influence, we will examine three effective formats (masterminds, mates, and mentors) in which such partnerships may occur. In fact, the most effective leaders leverage all three for maximum effect.

THE MASTERMIND

In his seminal book, *The Law of Success*, success guru Napoleon Hill highlights the words of one of the wealthiest men of his time, Andrew Carnegie, on the secret of success. Carnegie attributed it to the "sum total of the minds" of his business associates. Napoleon Hill coined the term "mastermind" to capture this collective synergy. Hill went on to convene an eclectic array of successful men into a mastermind group that is a collective Who's Who of influencers that transformed the business landscape.[125]

This synergistic power is not just reserved for the corporate setting. Famed writers C. S. Lewis (author of the famed Chronicles of Narnia series), J. R. R. Tolkien (author of the Lord of the Rings trilogy), as well as British poets Charles Williams and Owen Barfield, regularly convened in Oxford, England between 1933 and 1949 to stretch each other's creative works. They called themselves the Inklings.

Centuries earlier, in 1727, Benjamin Franklin brought together a group of men dubbed the Junto. Franklin describes the Junto as a "mutual improvement society" born of Franklin's love of conversation, personal development, philosophy, and politics. He attributes much of his prolific inventiveness to the Junto.[126]

Across centuries, geography, and industry, the pattern is self-evident. Great leaders, creative mavens, and people of profound influence without fail attribute their success to synergistic engagement with like-minded others. Your own success as a influencer will be tremendously bolstered by your ability to regularly connect with other influencers.

I currently belong to two mastermind groups. One of them I started for just this purpose. My mastermind group is called "The Influentials"—fitting, right? The Influentials is a group of high achievers who seek to encourage each other to increase the impact of our respective businesses and ministries. I have been extremely encouraged by rubbing shoulders with this group. The Bible assures us that "iron sharpens iron" (Proverbs 27:17). I cannot overemphasize the importance of having an encouragement network that pushes you to reach your goals, but

---

[125] Hill, N., *The Law of Success In Sixteen Lessons by Napoleon Hill*. 2011: Wilder Publications.

[126] About the Oviedo Junto Society. 2013 [cited 2015]; Available from: http://oviedojunto.org/about-the-oviedo-junto-society-2/.

also encourages you along the way. Of course, in my mastermind group, we share each other's content with our respective audiences and we introduce each other to key contacts. The idea is that my personal network becomes a shared network with The Influentials. We do this for each other. It is a form of shared partnership. So, it is no wonder that mastermind groups are increasingly becoming a must-have for creative influencers.

There are plenty of resources available online if you are interested in joining, or even starting, your own mastermind group. With the power of the Internet, these groups can be just as successful virtually as they are in person. The key to success lies in the people who are part of the group, the structure of the discussion, and the consistency of the meetings. Make the best effort to recruit people who are at various levels of achievement. But, be careful not to recruit those who are too far ahead of or behind everyone else. In order to maximize the benefit, have a defined, yet flexible agenda that encourages sharing and accountability. Finally, keep a regular schedule (at least once a month) and communicate the importance of attendance. Joining a mastermind group holds tremendous potential for you for sharing ingenuity with like-minded others.

MATES

In addition to mastermind groups, sometimes peer relationships offer ample accountability to effectively influence your path. One of the lessons that I have learned over the past several years is the importance of joining forces with people of similar passions and goals in order to build your respective brands.

I think back to when I wrote my first book, *Marriage ROCKS for Christian Couples*. A friend of mine and former seminary classmate, Joanne Weidman, amazed me with the level of commitment that she gave to the deep editing of the manuscript. She spent countless hours on this project. Indeed, I feel forever indebted to her doing this and not asking for a single penny to do so. This is the power of mates. The help that Joanne provided me was invaluable at that point in my journey. But, there is a larger point. Through her willingness to help me, our relationship became much more than editing and revisions. Our friendship and trust deepened. Years have now passed since that book was published. But, Joanne is a mate for life. I will do anything that I can to be there for her, as she was for me. A partnership does not have to be formal for it to be favored.

However, there are times when neglecting to legally define your relationship with mates is unwise — particularly where financial resources are at stake. In these instances, partnerships are formal legal entities where some percentage of the business (and profits) is shared. The contribution of each party to the agreement and roles are well-defined. As you grow your business or ministry endeavors, these types of mates become increasingly important.

> A common error that nascent platform builders make is trying to do everything themselves.

In addition to partners who become part of your endeavor, there are also times when you need mates for hire. There are contract employees and virtual assistants who are hired for projects or on retainer to complete ongoing tasks. There are organizations to which you can outsource vital or mundane tasks on your docket. Some common examples include services like Upwork, where you can hire someone for practically any category of project. There are websites like Fiverr.com and 99designs.com where graphic developers can be summoned at the click of a mouse. There are services such as legalzoom.com that can handle most aspects of your legal business documents. The list goes on and on. The main point here is that building your platform, especially on the second shift, requires that you selectively outsource tasks so that you can stay focused on the work that only you can do. This allows you to make the most productive use of your time.

A common error that nascent platform builders make is trying to do everything themselves—either to save money or to keep all of the details under their own control. The result is stymied growth in your efforts because you face time bottlenecks. You need to identify trusted people who share your level of excellence, adhere to deadlines, and support your vision. It is also important to consider partnerships with others who have a skill set or network reach that you do not. This is another way of extending your reach. In this way, you can effectively barter your respective skills and network to help each other.

When you find potential partners, treasure them and look for ways to sow into their passions as well. Some of these people will be long-term members of your team. Others will only serve short-term roles. Regardless, think of yourself as a team leader with the responsibility to bring out the best in each person with whom you partner. Do not just think about creating the best situation for yourself. Rather, consider arrangements where the felt needs and goals of team members are respected.

THE MENTORS

The final type of partnership to promote is the mentoring relationship. Mentoring is sharing the best of yourself to encourage the best in someone else. Mentoring is personal. Earlier, we saw the importance of Barnabas' partnership with Paul as they braved the challenges of winning Christian converts. But, there is another vital relationship that Paul cultivated over the course of his missionary work. That was a mentoring relationship with Timothy. With Paul's mentoring, Timothy became a major player in the effectiveness of the early Christian Church in spreading the Good News.

For many years of my adult life, I hoped and even prayed for an expert who would serve as a mentor—someone who would recognize my tremendous potential and choose to invest time in helping me develop. Or maybe it would be the perfect self-help book that would show me the clear path to my goals. Unfortunately, it does not seem to work that way. That desire never manifested, at least not in the way that I was thinking.

Eventually, however, I began to see that there were many virtual mentors that were available to me through the Internet, books, and podcasting. Unfortunately, so many people sit by too long, waiting for a mentor to appear, before they take action. They best heed the ancient Chinese proverb: "when the student is ready, the teacher will come." But, be open-minded because that teacher may look different than you expect. The question is whether you are ready to really listen for insight and wisdom.

Redemptive leaders have learned to not do it alone. It took me too long to understand this lesson, though others tried to tell me. Whether through masterminds, mates, or mentors, redemptive leaders actively look for opportunities to partner with people of shared passion and vision. God will show you your partners if you pay attention. Just take it slow. Be prayerful. Listen.

CHAPTER 22

FROM FIGHT TO FINISH

"Every soldier must know, before he goes into battle, how the little battle he is to fight fits into the larger picture, and how the success of his fighting will influence the battle as a whole."

–BERNARD LAW MONTGOMERY

Within each of us lies a quest. It isn't there by choice. It is there by design—placed by the Creator. The experiences and aspirations of your life have prepared you to be the hero of this journey. In that sense, this quest is not too big for you. You are at a crossroads that is likely to be a defining moment in the direction of your life. One path is acceptance of the status quo. Its appeal lies in its familiarity and predictability. It appeals to that core part of your brain that brandishes security like a medal of honor. There is, however, another path that challenges many of the assumptions of your past. It is a path of unprecedented growth and influence. But, for most of us, it appears too risky to embrace.

This book has been focused on your chosen path and how to best navigate it to wield extraordinary influence in our culture. Historically, many people have allowed their second-shift status to determine which path to choose. The challenges that the second shift presents for managing time, relationships, and resources are significant. Some days, it can get the best of you. It can derail even the most noble quest. But, there is one key thing to remember as you mull over your options: while you are the hero of the journey, the quest is ultimately not about you. The quest existed before you. You were just born to fulfill it.

> Your passion to do good works and wield extraordinary influence emanates from a divine source.

If we look thoughtfully at historical examples, we can see this clearly. Martin Luther King, Jr.'s journey—from pastor of a local Atlanta church to recipient of the Nobel Peace Prize in 1964—was about advancing the civil rights of African-American people. Abraham Lincoln's jaunt—from Illinois congressman to President of the United States—was about unifying a fragmented amalgam of states to form "a more perfect union." Of course, the central dividing issue was slavery. The Apostle Paul's conversion—from persecutor of the Church to its most prolific missionary—was not about him. It was about introducing the Gentile nations to the gospel of Christ. These are but three of practically innumerable examples. But, each of these stories points us to that central truth that your passion to do good works and wield extraordinary influence emanates from a divine source to fulfill His will on Earth. This truth underscores the fact that every noble calling is about the Creator's compassion for the plight of real people.

> God's intended direction for your life is charted along a spiritual map that only your GODprint senses.

It is liberating to know, especially when things are very challenging, that this race you undertake is not really about you — at least not mostly. Rather, it is about those whom you are called to engage — whether that is thousands of people or just one. Each of those lives is equally important and each depends on you running your race. God's plan for your life is not about the quantity of your reach. Rather, it is tapping into your bee nature and obediently demonstrating your creativity along your journey as a builder, aesthetic, advocate, or networker in spite of the DRAGONS. As Mother Teresa commented, "I have never had clarity; what I have always had is trust."[127] You see, it isn't about clarity of your path. It is about dogged obedience to your GODprint as you listen, love, and lead with extraordinary influence and a KINGDOM mindset.

Whether your influence remains primarily a second-shift endeavor or whether it eventually transitions to the first shift, the Creator gives the same instruction to run your race at your own pace with passion, attitude, creativity, and engagement. In reality, the first and second shifts are human-contrived concepts to account for chronological time. But, as we learned earlier, there are two time zones — physical and spiritual. God's intended direction for your life is charted along a spiritual map that only your GODprint senses.

We started off speaking of part-time passion and how to convert that to full-time influence. While that is an idea with intuitive appeal, with our richer understanding of influence we can see that, in actuality, it is the wrong starting point. Part-time passion is an apparition. There is no such thing in spiritual time. All purposeful passion flows from a divine source. That is its authority. The only question is your response to passion's push. Will you muster the will to listen emphatically, love wholeheartedly, and lead redemptively, so that you obediently

[127] Berry, C., "Jesuit Philosopher Recounts Time with Mother Teresa." Available from: http://www.catholiceducation.org/en/faith-and-character/faith-and-character/jesuit-philosopher-recounts-time-with-mother-teresa.html

create communities of exceptional influence in every aspect of your life? This selfless service is your highest calling because it prioritizes service to God and others above all else.

> Wholly commit yourself to the fight for your passion.

Throughout this book, we have used the Apostle Paul as an avatar for the journey that we all are called to create. We have followed his journey from reviled persecutor of the early Church to one of its staunchest proponents. It took a supernatural intervention to command that he really listen to God. But, once he did, he demonstrated an unquenchable love for God and the imperative to become that love for himself and others. As is the case with others, Paul's journey was not about him. Rather, it was about leadership that he developed in the early Church through the sermons he spoke, the people he trained, and the letters that he wrote (that still guide our Christian experiences, centuries after they were originally penned). Paul is credited with writing half of the Bible's New Testament (at least thirteen of the twenty-six books).

As Paul sensed that he was nearing the end of his journey, he penned a letter to Timothy in which he proudly states, "I have fought the good fight, I have finished the race, I have kept the faith" (2 Timothy 4:7). This book suggests a framework for extraordinary influence. But, ultimately, Paul's powerful words may succinctly encapsulate it all. Wholly commit yourself to the fight for your passion. Whether on the first or second shift, be the bee and fertilize your surroundings. But, there is something about Paul's assertion that his course is finished that captivates us all. It is in that sense that his purpose has been fulfilled. Despite the forces that sought to stop or minimize Paul's exploits, he creatively willed himself to the finish line— becoming what he described as all things to all people so that he might win some. When your eyes dim, will you be able to echo Paul's words? Will you run at your own pace and finish what your GODprint has started in you?

Finally, Paul instructs us that both the fight and the finish are faith-laden endeavors. Faith ties it all together. Those are the words with which I leave you. Ultimately, what it takes to have extraordinary influence is the will to consistently fight to follow your GODprint to its finish. Only your faith will sustain you through the lean periods and keep you centered during the times of excess. Your faith reminds you that this is really God's work for His people and purposes. You are simply an agent of the change God is cultivating. And, as with any agent, you are a representative of its culture.

You are created for influence.

ABOUT THE AUTHOR

Dr. Harold L. Arnold, Jr., Founder of The Pursuit of Influence, is a master of Second Shift influence. With a Ph.D. in Social and Organizational Psychology, Master's degree in Marriage and Family Therapy, and a Master's in Systems Engineering, Dr. Harold leverages his knowledge of business, social, and social systems to help leaders develop their deepest passions into robust spheres of influence. On his Second Shift, Dr. Harold writes and speaks extensively on family relationships and leadership development. He is also author of *Marriage ROCKS for Christian Couples.*

His favorite hobbies include watching good movies, reading good books, experiencing different cultures, and getting in some cardiovascular workouts.

ONLINE PLATFORMS:
Website/Blog: HaroldArnold.com, SecondShiftBook.com
Facebook: facebook.com/hlarnold
Twitter: @DrHaroldArnold
Email: Harold@HaroldArnold.com